BASEBALL COMPLETE

(Photo by William C. Greene, World-Telegram.)

George Herman (Babe) Ruth, ex-Yankee outfielder and champion
home-run hitter of all time. His eyes were so keen that he could
read the license numbers of an automobile so far away that others
could not even make out the colors of the plate (*see page 141*).

The late Lou Gehrig, iron-man first baseman for the Yankees, played in 2,130 consecutive games. Always a great hitter, Gehrig worked many extra hours on his fielding technique (*see page 59*).

(*Acme Photo.*)

In 1941 DiMaggio shattered all consecutive game-hitting records by batting safely in 56 straight contests. Here, in the middle of that hitting streak, he bats against the St. Louis Browns on June 26. Note the long stride and easy stance, and, in the background, the avid attention of teammates.

The spotlight was on Robinson as the first Negro to play in a World Series.

RUSS HODGES

BASEBALL
COMPLETE

The Big League  Baseball Library

GROSSET & DUNLAP *Publishers*
NEW YORK

PUBLISHED BY ARRANGEMENT WITH RUDOLPH FIELD

PRINTED IN THE UNITED STATES OF AMERICA

Table of Contents

Foreword by Jimmy Powers

Sometime ago, I wrote a book. It was called "Baseball Personalities." As books go, this one went pretty well. It sold better than average, which of course is better than average. Now my old friend Russ Hodges has written a book. This is good. I mean it, the book is good.

Not so long ago, book publishers everywhere were moaning the blues. No book was selling and no publisher was making a dime. "What's the trouble?" asked the publishing clan. "Why aren't more people reading books?"

A newspaper brother of mine supplied the answer when he said succinctly, "Nobody is reading books because everybody is so busy writing them."

Be that as it may, Russ Hodges still had a book to get out of his system. That he did a noble chore will be proved by the rush to the bookstalls as soon as his "Baseball Complete" comes roaring off the presses. I predict a healthy sale for "Baseball Complete" and for Russ's sake, I'm happy indeed about the whole thing.

"Baseball Complete," allow me to report, is made to order for the real, rabid American baseball fan. To Russ's credit, he far from eulogizes every name connected with baseball. For every world-beater you read about, you'll learn the sad saga of some diamond deadbeat. Hodges never pulled his punches and he doesn't in "Baseball Complete."

The chapter on sports oddities I found exceptionally entertaining. We writers of the dot-and-dash feature column are always on the lookout for the unusual in sports, as you probably have noticed. "Baseball Complete" does a grand job in bringing you a solid collection of baseball's biggest believe-it-or-not items. You'll be astounded—like I was—at some of the most lopsided scores in the history of baseball, some of the game's best-pitched contests and some of the most terrific batting bonanzas. It's always interesting to note how some of the diamond's most unbelievable records are held by less famous performers.

Good for a hearty, healthy chuckle is the chapter on baseball humor, stories never before told in such sparkling fashion.

All too often, we take our daily baseball much too seriously. Heated arguments and lifelong hates have developed over diamond controversies. Managers of big-league clubs have been victimized with more abuse than a fascist dictator for blowing a lone, solitary ballgame out of a possible 162. Umpires have been threatened with the torture chamber.

Then why not a few laughs from the grandstand? The only criticism I have with the Hodges chapter on humor is it's not enough. We could do with an entire book on the subject. Notwithstanding, Russ the writer has rounded up a socko selection of yaks and if you don't roar at cracks like the one by famed Wilbert Robinson, "Over-confidence may yet cost the Dodgers sixth place," then you're nothing but a six o'clock grouch.

Careful consideration brings to mind all too few of baseball's funny men. Today, we have great cards like Frankie Frisch and Yogi Berra, while yesterday the bonafide buffoons consisted of gents like Wilbert Robinson, Babe Ruth, Babe Herman and Lefty Gomez. There were others and some guys who were funny without trying to be. But as in most walks of life, the serious ones far outnumber the happy-go-lucky persons and their stories are thrilling.

I could talk about all chapters of "Baseball Complete." Each one contains a nugget of gold, but you can dig them out as you read the book. Of real interest is the chapter on ballplayers who could have possibly been as great as the greatest, except for one flaw in their physical or mental makeups. It's interesting to read about these men and speculate about what might have happened had they possessed that little extra spark. It's also fun figuring about how success on the part of these failures might have meant one or more pennants to a team, thereby changing entirely the history of the game.

Before I finish this piece, I want to say one more thing about Russ's book, "Baseball Complete." Read it and enjoy it. Have fun, folks. It's a grand baseball book.

Introduction by Russ Hodges

At first this was to have been a book about an outstanding sports personality. We were going to pick one of today's biggest diamond sparklers, turn him inside out and dissect him for the fans. Naturally, we got to thinking about whom to profile in such fashion. Names and more names ran through our mind, day and night. Stars past and present paraded through our dreams.

"How about Ted Williams? How about Wee Willie

Keeler? How about Frankie Frisch?" Every friend had
a suggestion to make. None appealed, particularly.

For quite some years now we have been covering
the sports front vocally with emphasis on baseball.
Day in, day out we have observed outstanding and
interesting feats of prowess on the infield and outfield grass. Why not a roundup of baseball happenings, we wondered? Besides, we argued with ourself
in convincing fashion, people are always writing or
calling to ask a question about baseball history, past
and present.

We'd do it! We'd set aside the microphone after a
day's (or night's) work and start tapping out a tempo
on the typewriter. We'd set down as many facts and
figures on diamond doings and personalities as we
could possibly cram into one column. Instead of de-
voting several pages to any one incident, we'd try to
spread a number of occurrences over one page, when
feasible. That, we decided, was what the fans wanted
most.

At first we spent little time in front of the typewriter. Most of the early months of our tidbit was de-
voted to research. We dug deep for facts everywhere
—musty magazines, beat-up books, knocked-about
newspapers and we buttonholed friend and foe alike
to get his favorite baseball yarn. At times, we even
back-tracked down our own memory lane.

"Thanks a million," we say to fellows like Jack
Schwartz, the publisher of "Grandstand Manager,"
the fan publication of the old New York Giants. Senor
Schwartz is a collector without peer of published
pages on baseball. Jack has chronicled much of this

information in his "Grandstand Manager" and we found the zippy monthly sheet a fountain of inspiration. There are others, of course, who helped, but space does not permit. So, allow us just to say: "We thank you one and all."

Whenever a guy writes a book, he usually says he came across so much data he had to leave nine-tenths of the stuff out. We didn't. As we started to say a dozen paragraphs earlier, we made an effort to pack in as much fact and figure as the poor book would hold, and we did. Hence, we can honestly admit we tossed aside very few lines. In cases where we exercised doubt as to the authenticity of a yarn, we cut. Otherwise, everything (of interest) went in. As a result, we think you'll find "Baseball Complete" a handy reference guide besides a book full of stories, happenings and opinions.

You know, sitting in the broadcasting or television booth, I've always envied those newspaper guys. They make a mistake and they correct it. In broadcasting, we let the tongue slip and a half-hundred fans let us know about it. You've heard the old wheeze about the grass always looking greener on the other side of the infield. Now we're not so sure. Writing is hard work. We admit it. Sometimes on the air, we talk ourself dizzy, but we learned that the typewriter, too, can make your head spin. And while we broadcasting guys are rarely at a loss for words, sometimes that typewriter just won't produce a decent sounding phrase.

Confidentially, we think we'll stick to broadcasting. (Maybe after reading this book, everybody will chant in chorus: "We hope he does!")

To give all the fans a break while writing a book

is harder than appears on the surface. Suppose, for example, you get hot on the subject of the Detroit Tigers. One topic leads to another and pretty soon you find yourself writing a chapter on the Bengals. Naturally, this does not please the followers of the Phillies, the White Sox or the Chicago Cubs. You must stop yourself short and give some thought to the other 19 clubs in the majors. Things like this slow up operations and make the writing of a book even tougher.

Another problem is the weak sister club of the league. Both the American and National Leagues have had teams which dominated the play throughout most of the seasons and naturally such ball clubs have produced the greatest number of star players. No baseball history can be complete without mentioning headline heroes like Ty Cobb, Rogers Hornsby, Joe DiMaggio, Babe Ruth, Christy Mathewson, and practically the entire congregation of the Hall of Fame. You know many scribes before you have written the exploits of these diamond dandies, yet you must mention them and their feats again. The same applies to the great ball clubs like Connie Mack's prolific pennant-snatching Athletics of yesterday's generation and of McGraw's Giants. Baseball's greatest drama has been produced usually during World Series competition when the sports pages of the entire nation are given over to the championships of the National Pastime.

Well, we've talked enough about our great hardship which has become "Baseball Complete." If, perchance, you should find our blood, sweat and tears of some enjoyment you'll be erasing all of the pain.

Happy reading!

Greater Than The Great

For years, sports fans talked about the man who might someday come along and break Babe Ruth's mighty record of 60 homers in one year. It was one of baseball's longest standing marks and one of the most cherished records of the game. Many fans hoped that no one would ever erase that mark from the books. Many candidates came close. There were Greenberg and Foxx, both of whom smacked 58 in a single season. Ralph Kiner had his cheerleaders, and more recently, Willie Mays, Hank Aaron and Mickey Mantle all looked like they might break the magic mark. But it remained for an angry young Yankee who in 1961 had himself a year of years to finally became the first player in major league history to produce a greater homer output for a single season than even Babe Ruth. The man was Roger Maris.

Experts will probably always disagree about whether Roger should have a line alone in the record books, or whether his new record should be marked with an asterisk. The Babe hit his 60 in a 154 game season. Maris managed 61 in 162 games.

A number of seasons back, there was one man who never came close to breaking the Babe's mark, though experts at the time gave him a solid chance to become a record breaker. His name was Vince DiMaggio, a brother of the famous Joe. Participating in 157 games for the Pirates in 1943, Vince didn't make the experts look too good by batting a meek .248 and hitting 15 home runs.

The last memory of brother Vince as a big leaguer revolves around his brief tenure with the New York Giants where he produced nary a base hit and finally packed up and made off for pleasanter pastures out on the Pacific coast. Afflicted with a severe case of hole-in-the-bat, Vince set more whiffing records than slugging marks, though he did manage to cut out a slugging space for himself in the record books. Vince DiMaggio you see is one of a quartet of major leaguers who has rapped four home runs during a single season with the sacks clogged with runners. He did it in 1945 while wearing a Philadelphia Philly uniform. Vince never made much progress before or after that season, but who can deny he pelted the pill as hard as any man ever to swing a bat over home plate.

Maybe Vince didn't concentrate hard enough. Some good hitters are made, not born. Take a yeoman stickman like Hank Greenberg. So anxious was the Big Bronx Boy to make the grade in the big show he hustled out to Briggs Stadium, Detroit, every morning at dawn swinging a bat until he knocked the kinks out of his cut. It took all the patience of Joe Cronin, then Red Sox manager, to restrain Ted Williams from trying to pulverize every shoulder-high pitch within waving range. Before Cronin took Ted in tow, the slamming splinter batted the breeze 64 times during his first big-time campaign.

To be sure, Vince had able instructors at his elbows—one on each side in the persons of Joe and Dominic DiMaggio. It could have been just a case of where Vince didn't have the natural batting eye. Temperament in a ball player can often be the decisive factor.

Ask the Yankees. They lost two star pitchers, Charley Devens of Harvard and Johnny Broaca of Yale, because the boys simply sizzled at club policy and walked out forever on baseball.

In Vince DiMaggio's case he was all baseball, a guy who gave it his all and who put every ounce of energy into the game whether at bat or afield where he was much better than average. Nobody ever tried harder to hit the ball harder than Vince DiMaggio during the 1938 season with the Braves. Vince, however, had the misfortune to end up the season by batting the breeze four times against Giant chucker Harry Gumbert. Casey Stengel, brave Braves manager, threw up his hat in despair for Vince had set a new major-league whiff mark of 134 in 150 games, so Case shuttled off Vince to Kansas City along with a bunch of other Braves to acquire shortstop Eddie Miller.

Boston it seems has had its share of striker-outers. A year after Vince set the high waving figure, rookie outfielder Chet Ross almost duplicated it by taking three futile swings exactly 127 times. Like V. DiMag, Ross also showed plate power by blasting 17 home runs. Unfortunately for the Braves, Ross too never lived up to early promise but it took a tough break—a broken fibula—to stop him. He sprained his ankle sliding during the spring training campaign of 1941, then in mid-July of the same season he fractured the fibula. That was just about all for unlucky Chet.

"Greatest outfielder since Joe DiMaggio," sages said as Harold Pete Reiser became a Brooklyn Dodger regular in 1941. Pete had everything, a good eye, batting power, tremendous speed and a wonderful throwing arm. Living up to advance notices, Pete smacked the ball for a league-leading .343 average, the first rookie to capture the honor. His work in the outfield was just as good, highlighted by daring, sparkling catches, while on the base paths he was the scourge of the league, swiping 20 sacks.

The beginning of a slow end began for Pete Reiser in the second game of a mid-season 1942 double-header in Sportsman's park, St. Louis, as the Dodgers battled to beat off the challenging Cardinals. Down to the last of the eleventh the teams were tied 6-6 until the mighty Country Slaughter stepped to the plate. The hard-driving Card outer-gardener slammed a long fly ball to deep center. Always the hard competitor, Reiser turned and chased the ball with flying feet. He caught up with the ball just as his head caught up with the concrete wall; Pete had the ball in his grasp but it trickled slowly to the grass as Pete collapsed on the field. Racing around the bases, Enos Slaughter scored the winning run. A few minutes later they rushed Pete in an ambulance to the hospital with a brain concussion.

A hard guy to keep in a hospital bed, Reiser rapidly took up his outfield post again but never with the same efficiency. From league-leading batter, his average fell off 50 points and Pete eventually finished the season with .310. Headaches and dizzy spells plagued Reiser, never to disappear completely, and his return from the wars in 1946 saw Pistol Pete peck for a disappointing .277 in 122 games. His speed, on the other hand, never deserted him, for during this same 1946 season he swiped all of 34 bases.

But bad luck kept so close to Pistol Pete's elbow it affected his throwing arm to a degree where shortstop PeeWee Reese would charge halfway to the outfield to give the one-time rapid rifle an assist on every throw-in. In 1949 Reiser donned the uniform of the Boston Braves, retrogressing again this time to .272 in 84 games. And in 1950, used chiefly as a pinch-hitter, Harold Reiser had trouble keeping his head above the .200 mark. Shortly after the season closed, the Braves asked waivers on the one-time great outfield prospect.

Can a player with so much original promise possibly be washed up at a time which should be the height of his career? Harold Pete Reiser was never able to rebound and fulfill the promise of becoming the greatest outfielder since DiMaggio.

Who do you think smacked the hardest ball in baseball history? First guess would seem to be some muscle man like Hack Wilson, Jimmy Foxx, Chuck Klein or Babe Ruth. First guess, however, would probably be wrong. Those who have seen him hit insist nobody generated more power than Dale Alexander. One of the worst flychasers in the history of baseball, Dale never did make it big in the big leagues.

Alexander could put wicked wood to horsehide and this was proved in a game he played with Toronto against Jersey City in the International League. Over in Jersey they still talk about it. Dale drilled a liner so hard it made as much noise smacking into the mitt of Jersey right-fielder Ed Kunesh as it did leaving Alexander's bat. Kunesh carried that baseball back to his dugout; he wanted to prove something to his Jersey teammates. As everybody on the bench gaped, Kunesh displayed a baseball actually knocked lopsided by Dale Alexander's blow. Unfortunately for Dale, however, he lacked the grace to go with his gusto.

Back in 1929, the Tigers apparently had heard of Dale Alexander's mucho gusto for they laid $100,000 on the line plus three players for Alexander and a pitcher whose name escapes memory. Everybody knew about Dale Alexander; he could hit with horsepower, but he fielded with a prayer. In desperation, Detroit at length sent Dale to the Red Sox in a swap for outfielder Earl Webb.

In beantown surroundings Dale Alexander came to life and he must have been a solid disappointment to Jimmy Foxx of the Athletics, for old double-XX was having one of his finest seasons. The 1929 semester saw Foxx perform such incredible feats as batting for 438 total bases, blasting out 58 home runs and driving in 169 runners. Yet, the honor that would have given Jimmy a grand slam escaped his grasp and fell to a rival first-baseman, Dale Alexander of the Red Sox. That's the season Alexander led all American League hitters with a .367 while Jimmy Foxx fell just short of the title with a .364.

The following season a bad leg hampered Dale Alexander and he missed many games. He never again recaptured his 1932 batting ability.

In 1916 a pitcher named Ferdie Schupp, a left-hander, was a guy with a world of puzzling stuff. In several previous seasons, Schupp had been hardly any

puzzle at all and visiting teams to the Polo Grounds
loved to level off at the slants of this relief hurler.
Then along about the middle of 1916, Ferdie did an
abrupt about-face to compile the best earned-run average in the majors, a staggering .090. The following
season Schupp did even better by posting 21 victories for the Giants and spinning a tidy shutout, a
seven-hit, 5-0 game to win one of the two victories in
a 4-2 Giant trouncing at the hands of the White Sox
in the World Series.

In his first start of the series, Schupp sought the
showers early as he was batted out in the second inning, the White Sox going on to a 7-2 victory. However, Schupp was not charged with the loss. Ferdie
Schupp then went into the World War I army and returned empty-handed, without his stuff. The Cardinals took a gamble on the left-hander, but could never
make him a big winner.

Everybody knows the strikeout artistry of Walter
Johnson but who remembers the whiff wizardry of
Swifty Johnson? Well, baseball history records the
fine 1912 afternoon that 15-year-old Swifty was on the
mound for the Wilkins team of the Braddock City,
Pennsylvania League, the afternoon Swifty fanned
24 Patton batsmen in nine regulation innings. Actu-
ally, Swifty started stronger, for of the first 15 batters
Johnson pitched to he set down 14 on strikes. Swifty
Johnson, by the way, was said to be a cousin of Walter
Johnson but the former never achieved the Big Train's
fame and fortune.

On August 4, 1945, Hal Gregg of Brooklyn pitched
a no-hit game against the Boston Braves for seven full

innings until, as was his wont, Joe Medwick cut at a very bad ball and lined a single to left for the only hit off Hal. Bad back and all, young Gregg looked to be the best Dodger hurling discovery since Whitlow Wyatt. In 1946, the very next season, Gregg flopped hard, winning six and losing four with a second-place team and in time he drifted to Pittsburgh, then out of the league.

Tom McBride is not nearly as famous a Boston Red Soxer as Ted Williams, but he holds a slugging record never equalled by the splendorous splinter. On the very same day Hal Gregg was spinning his one-hitter, Tom McBride was going down in baseball annals along with such notables of knock as Fred Merkle of the 1911 Giants and Bob Johnson of the 1937 Athletics.

Here's how Tom accomplished his feat. Coming up with the bases loaded, he slammed a solid two bagger to clear the sacks. Later in the same inning, Tom McBride stepped into the batter's box again and once more the bases were congested. This time Tom did even better. He took one mighty swing, smiting a triple and clearing the sacks of Sox to drive home three more runs. Thus between the span of outs, none and three, Tom McBride hammered home six runs to tie an all-time mark. How many more famous major-league sluggers can come close to Tom McBride's mark?

No less an authority than Spud Chandler, distinguished Yankee mound ace, declared, "Bill Zuber can throw a baseball harder than Bob Feller." Nevertheless, in a mediocre career in the majors, Bill Zuber never compiled much of a mark. Who can say why? In 1945, Zuber won five games for the Yankees, lost eleven. To be sure, Zuber was often a victim of circumstances. Starting 12 games during that season, big Bill was dismayed to see his Yankee mates get him nary a run in seven of those contests. Bill begged for runs but all he ever got was loud outs.

Zuber came to the big leagues with Cleveland in 1936 and departed from Boston in 1947. Never during any single season did Bill win as many as ten games. That Bill Zuber could pitch on occasion was proved in 1942 when he took the hill for lowly Washington against pennant-bound New York to stop the mighty McCarthymen 1-0.

Zuber was the kind of hurler who could rear back and throw the ball through a hitter if he chose. But Bill was short on baseball savvy. No puzzling variety of serves had he and fielding his position slickly was beyond Bill.

It was back in August, 1937, that two young, highly heralded rookie pitchers took the mound opposite one another, each making his major-league debut and each without previous farm-club experience. One of the hurlers was Bobbie Feller, an 18-year-old upstart from an Iowa farm while his opponent was Newton (Bucky) Jacobs, a cute curve-baller of no-run, no-hit fame down at the University of Richmond. The papers made much of this pitching rubber match between the freshmen and a curious crowd turned out to see Feller & Co., better known as the Cleveland Indians, turn back Washington 11-2 by knocking the college kid from the hill early.

"They really didn't give me a chance," Bucky Jacobs was quoted as saying in later years. "I started once and then nothing but a steady diet of relief. To be effective, I had to take my regular turn on the mound."

Who knows how far Bucky might have gone had he taken that regular mound chore? It was much to Bucky's misfortune that he drew the talents of Rapid Robert Feller in his big-time inaugural.

Dizzy Dean always insisted that his brother Paul could throw a baseball harder than could ole Diz, the great one, himself. Many observers agreed, for when Paul poured through the high hard one he blinded the best batters. However, Paul never had Dizzy's assortment of serves and when his hop didn't, Paul was through. Now, if Paul had possessed the temperament, confidence and general physical makeup of Dizzy Dean, well there could have been another Dean candidate for the Hall of Fame. But quiet, retiring Paul Dean just wasn't fated to attain Dizzy's bombastic prominence.

Brooklyn fans will never forget the fall doubleheader of the 1934 season when the Cards came to town, played the Brooks a twin ball and shut out the locals 13-0 and 3-0. Dizzy Dean achieved the whitewashing in the first contest by giving up his first hit as late as the eighth inning but brother Paul came on to improve even on Dizzy's performance. He turned the Dodgers back without anything resembling a hit and there are those who were in the stands that day who will always maintain that Paul, at his best, was a better hurler than the incomparable Dizzy.

"Paul was even greater than Ole Diz," remarked Dizzy Dean modestly on the occasion.

Greatness in baseball usually is measured in the same way as in other business ventures, in cold cash, that is. When you think of the big money players of baseball you always get around to the fabulous salaries of guys like Babe Ruth, Joe DiMaggio, Bob Feller, and Ted Williams. Yet, dollar for dollar, there's another money man who ranks right up with the top quartet, at least percentage-wise. He's former Yankee shortstop Frankie Crosetti.

Impossible, you say, but wait. After joining the New York Yankees in 1932, Frankie the flea appeared in no less than eight World Series, earning him a total of exactly $44,631.98. How many other big-league players earned such a sum for so few games? Hardly any!

Had he been able to do so much as catch a fly ball, Smead Jolley might easily have been as immortal a ball player as Tris Speaker, Bill Terry or Honus Wagner. As it was, however, Jolley never did learn to basket a can of corn and his career in the majors as a result covered a span of less than five seasons. Watching Smead fall flat on his face chasing fly balls for Chicago in Comiskey Park and for the Red Sox in Fenway Park led one wag to comment, "You are looking at the poor man's Babe Herman."

No doubt Smead Jolley had the ability to become one of baseball's greatest hitters if he had not been handicapped mentally by the knowledge he let in as many runs as he batted in. What slugging star, including Ty Cobb, Wagner, Stan Musial, et al, could boast a minor-league hitting record to approach Jolley's? In five seasons with San Francisco of the Pacific Coast League, Smead smacked out such averages as .447, .404, .397, .387, and .346. (The latter mark must have struck Jolley as disastrous.)

Although his hitting with the White Sox was below his minor-league par, Smead Jolley did manage to post percentages like .313 and .309. Completely discouraged of ever making an acceptable fielder of Jolley, the White Sox at length peddled Smead to the Red Sox who tried to make the gawky guy into a catcher with no success. During his 1932 season with the Boston club Jolley hit .312 and drove out 18 home runs.

Imagine the change, though, in today's record books had any manager been able to figure a way of improving Jolley's fielding. His minor-league confidence restored, there is no question that Smead would have gone down in baseball lore—at least in a more favorable light.

Probably you don't remember the name Johnny Miljus. He was a pitcher and he toiled for the Pirates during the twenties. However, those who saw Johnny in action in the 1927 World Series—Ruthian Yanks versus poor Pittsburgh—won't forget the fast ball flashed by this Pirate fireballer. He was wild and he lost a crucial game in the ninth but not one of the awesome Yanks hit him.

Making his appearance in the fourth Series game, played at the Yankee Stadium, Johnny Miljus was a last hope measure as the Yankees had taken the first three contests in a row behind the brilliant pitching of Hoyt, Moore, Pennock and Pipgras. In the fourth contest, Miljus took the hill in the bottom of the seventh after his mates had tied the score at 3-all in the top half of the inning. Through the seventh and eighth rounds, blaze-ball Johnny held the hammering Yanks in check but in the bottom of the ninth he was to exhibit a pitching performance that will be remembered forever in World Series conversation.

A pair of walks and bunt single loaded the bases with none out and it looked like quick curtains for Miljus and the Pirates. As Lou Gehrig stepped to the plate he put Miljus Johnny-on-the-spot. A cry of incredulity swept the big Stadium as Johnny whiffed Gehrig with hopping fast balls. Still, he seemed out of the pan into the pot as busting Bob Meusel waved a stick at Johnny from the batter's box. No Pittsburgh partisan dared even imagine what would happen next, but it did; Johnny Miljus fanned Bob Meusel.

Suddenly, Pirate rooters were gaining strength. Here was Tony Lazzeri and magnificent Miljus should handle him. Tony couldn't hit Miljus—and he didn't, largely because Poosh Em-Up lacked a ten-foot pole. The first delivery from pitcher Miljus sailed high over everybody's head and gained height until it plunked dully into the screen behind home plate. With ease, Earl Combs sprinted home from home plate and a four-game sweep of the Series for the Yankees.

What might have happened had Johnny Miljus stopped the Yanks in that crucial game is of course open to discussion. Surely, the Yanks seemed a cinch to wrap up the Fall Classic but with the confidence of an impressive victory under his belt, Johnny Miljus should have become a better pitcher. As it was, he never made many headlines although he had the equipment, a fast ball that took off, only sometimes it took off a little too much.

Back in the days before World War I, the Yankees had a ball player billed at various times as another "Ty Cobb." In later years, the Giants came up with Johnny Rucker, a speedy outfielder who off his performance in triple-A ball earned a similar title. However, as in the case of Rucker this earlier Cobb discovered he couldn't steal first base and he eventually left baseball. His name was Lee Magee and he could play anywhere—first, second, the outfield. Those who saw him perform with the Yanks—and previously with the Cards—called him the fastest thing on two feet. With the Yankees, Magee had the misfortune to break one of those valuable legs and that was that.

As a matter of fact, so many promising rookies have at one time or another earned the title "another Ty Cobb," but no one yet has really been "another Ty Cobb."

How many of today's new crop of baseball fans can identify Big Jim Vaughn? Not many, you may wager. Yet huge Hippo Vaughan piled up one of the best pitching marks in Chicago Cub history. From 1914 to 1919, the big lefty won 20 or more games per season, with one exception. In view of this truly remarkable record, it's startling to discover Hippo takes a back seat on the dugout to many more colorful and less talented players of his era.

Big Jim Vaughn missed the record books by the narrowest of margins back in 1917 against the Cincinnati Reds at Weeghman Park; that was before the

Cub home became known as Wrigley Field. For nine
innings on this spring afternoon, Vaughn pitched no-
run, no-hit ball but he lost the game in the tenth on a
solid single, a couple of errors and a bunt single. What
is even more unbelievable is the fact that Vaughn's
opponent, Cincy's Fred Toney also pitched a no-hit-
ter! And what is more, Toney turned back the Cubs
in the tenth to make a place for himself in baseball's
archives. Had Jim Vaughn's Cub mates got the burly
portsider at least a run that day during the regulation
nine innings, the big fellow would have unquestionably earned the lasting recognition he so warmly deserved.

There wasn't a more highly regarded pitcher in all
baseball than Johnny VanderMeer, not after the lightning lefty made diamond history by pitching two consecutive no-run, no-hit games, the first on June 11
against Boston and the second during a night game
at Brooklyn on June 15. All this happened in 1938
when Vandy won 15 while dropping ten for fourth-
place Cincinnati.

Like later arrivals, such as Brooklyn's fabulous Rex
Barney and the Yankees' Tommy Byrne, the big
Dutchman lacked control. When he had trouble finding the range, he sometimes aimed the ball down the
middle with disastrous results as big-league batters
pickled the fat fast one. The double-no-hit Vander-
Meer of 1938 never sparkled so brightly again although those who batted against the blond, strong-
armed southpaw claimed there never was another so
tough to hit.

The same comments were passed around about

Brooklyn Rex Barney as he turned back the Giants without a hit or run in a night game several seasons back. The Barney ball blazed over the plate fast enough to produce praise like, "He's faster than Feller." Maybe Rex was faster than Feller, but he was never able to match Roaring Robert's greatness because he could not point his pitches in the direction of home plate.

performances of World Series play was turned in by Rex against the Yankees in 1947. Because Manager Burt Shotton was short on pitchers he sent out Barney to start against the slugging Yankees. Rex rapidly lived up to his reputation, and in short order his wildness filled the sacks with nobody out. At this point, Rex somehow found the plate and he whiffed Joe DiMaggio. The next two batters, George McQuinn and Billy Johnson, went down on an easy foul fly and another strikeout and erratic Rex finished the wild round in a blaze of glory.

You take a guy and you ask him to win a ball game in which his teammates are doing everything in their power to lose. You really can't expect this pitcher to do much, so you are more than mildly surprised when he posts an extraordinary 3-0 victory. The only way he can win this one, you say, is for him to strike out every batter in the lineup which would make him the greatest pitcher in the history of baseball.

That's the way it was with little Dickie Kerr when he took the mound for the infamous Black Sox of Chicago against the Reds of Cincinnati in the World Series of 1919. The Sox had gone down to defeat twice with their two best moundsmen, Eddie Cicotte and

Al Williams, both performing in peculiar fashion on the hill, to say the least. In the third contest, Kerr, the lithe lefty, toed the rubber with an average 13-8 season record to his credit.

"What chance has Dickie when Cicotte and Williams got their lumps already?" scoffers sneered.

But little Dickie showed them by twirling three-hit baseball, walking only one man. What's more, he beat a good Cincinnati righthander, Ray Fisher, and the Black Sox committed not an error on the field.

Sure, the Sox were levelling for that one. Under the circumstances you couldn't really call Kerr the best in the business. Still, Dickie did win for a club which was not exactly knocking itself out for a victory so you have to take his chore at more than face value. Of greater import is the fact that Dickie Kerr did it again in the sixth game, beating Cincinnati 5-4 in ten innings and winning over ranking tossers like Walter Dutch Reuther, Red southpaw and reliable Jimmy Ring. Maybe a couple of his mates later did call Dickie Kerr a "busher," but the only thing he threw was a baseball, not a ball game!

In the eyes of Sid Mercer, the greatest shortstop of all time in baseball was one Bobby Wallace who starred with the old Cleveland team when they were known as the Spiders. This was before 1900 and during his 25th year of big-league play, Bobby was still on the job doing as capable a job as ever for the Cardinals. Had not Wallace been overshadowed by the all-around brilliance of Honus Wagner he would unquestionably be singled out today as the Mr. Shortstop of major-league baseball.

For sheer fielding ability however it would be hard to top one Everett Scott, Red Sox and Yankee shortstop. This agile gent led the American League in fielding for eight consecutive seasons.

Throughout the years, the frequently down-trodden St. Louis Browns have come up with more pitching hopefuls than the Stevens Brothers have hot dogs. No stickout Brownie hurler comes to mind quickly—the matter requires some thought. There was one Brownie who labored on the mound back in 1922 who could have been the greatest twirler in the history of the game had he pitched to none other than Babe Ruth three times per inning.

The young lefthander was Hubert (Shucks) Pruett and he was, to boot, a rookie direct from the University of Missouri. It is doubtful if one of Pruett's courses at Missouri was on how to pitch to Babe Ruth, but what this irrepressible kid did to the Bambino nobody before or after could come close to duplicating.

Shucks Pruett actually struck out the mighty Babe Ruth ten times in a row! Off his ability against baseball's best ball-basher, Pruett should have become the game's number-one pitcher. He never did and few today even recall his name.

Versatility Is A Virtue?

If Art (Wottaman) Shires hadn't taken to baseball, the husky first-sacker could have done just as well—if not better—at football. Shires actually played football at five different colleges and at all he earned his letter in spades. Next, Art took up boxing and showed he was just as handy a guy with the dukes. However, had Wottaman been able to fight a fight as well as he was able to talk a game of baseball, he might have fought Joe Louis to a standstill. He never got the chance!

Nobody who ever saw big George Magerkurth umpire a game could doubt that this pugnacious gent would have been a sensation in the ring and he actually was. Before his 21st birthday, gentleman George was fighting on Mississippi River piers and barges and it's said that he once chalked up an astonishing skein of 40 straight wins. A pity Leo Durocher and some others didn't know about this!

In his first season with the 1950 New York Yankees, blond and battering Jackie Jensen didn't show much besides a lot of muscle and hustle. Those who observed his play in the Pacific Coast League the previous season stamped Jackie as sure-thing big-league material. Green as grass, Jensen joined the Yanks much too soon because he was a bonus baby. At football, though, Jackie Jensen had few peers. One of California U.'s all-time greats, the blond bomber was the kind of fireball fullback who made All-American on every important team in the country.

Jackie's 1950 manager, Casey Stengel, felt certain

the California comet would make the grade. He let go of reliable Johnny Lindell to make a place on his nifty '50 squad for the raw righthanded recruit.

California, at that, seems to produce baseballing footballers in quantity as well as quality. For years Sam Chapman was Mr. Power of the Philadelphia Athletic outfield. For several years before joining the A.'s, Sam starred on the University of California gridiron. Chapman stood out on the powerhouse Trojan eleven of 1937 when he made All-American. Chapman also shone with the Athletics of 1941 when he socked the Spalding for an acceptable .321. After a hitch in the Navy as a flyer, Sam didn't do too well in figures, but he has in fact by knocking down droves of runs across the plate for the willow-weak Philadelphians. In 1946, shortly after Sam's release from service, he swatted the sphere for an uninspiring .261; however, the hustling outfielder did contrive to blast out 20 home runs and to account for 234 total bases.

Granted that Frankie Frisch was one of baseball's all-time infield greats, it should be remembered though that fuming Frankie came to the big leagues as the Fordham Flash—and a flashier fellow never dazzled followers of the football field. As a member of the Fordham backfield, fearless Franz could lug that leather as few before or after could.

"Greatest back in the history of Fordham football," are the words of authority, those of Ram trainer Jake Weber.

Leading Cincinnati hitter in the 1919 World Series against the Chicago Black Sox was an efficient outfielder by the name of Greasy Neale. Many folks today know of Greasy but many have forgotten his past baseball ability. As coach of the powerhouse Philadelphia Eagles of the National Football League, Neale has established an enviable reputation as a grid whiz. Getting back to Greasy's baseball prowess, well, in that infamous 1919 Series, Neale led all Cincinnati hitters with an average of .357.

At Oregon they still talk about the bruising blocks tossed by grid great Joe Gordon. The former Oregon backfielder is the same Flash Gordon who starred for years with the Yankees and later with Cleveland before shoving off for the Pacific Coast League and a manager's job. However, as a second-baseman in baseball, Gordon probably was on the receiving end of more bone-crushing blocks via attempts to break up double-plays than he ever dished out in college.

All the sports world remembers Nat Holman as coach of the CCNY double-champ Beavers basketball five, and older followers of court have heard Nat proclaimed the "world's greatest basketball player" during the days he performed for the original Celtics back in the '20s.

In truth, Nat was not an all-around athlete. At New York's Commerce High School he was an all-scholastic halfback and a ditto choice for the soccer squad. Yet it is not widely known that Nat was almost as good at baseball as at any of the aforementioned sports—perhaps better. As a pitcher and second-baseman for Commerce, he performed for a team that lost the city title by one game. As a matter of fact, Holman's diamond doings attracted such wide attention he was handed a contract to play with the Cincinnati Reds as soon as he exited from high school. Nat, though, chose basketball so he never had the opportunity to find out if he could become the "world's greatest baseball player," the title akin to the one he earned on the basketball court.

About a dozen years ago, Duke had a surplus of star halfbacks in Eric Tipton and Ace Parker. Both were All-American and are listed among the all-time greats of any grid diamond. Ace Parker, although a skinny 170 lbs. for football, was the Babe Ruth of the grid game when he played backfield for the Brooklyn football Dodgers. There are some experts who call him the best ever.

Ace Parker seemed like a promising Pittsburgh Pirate infielder but his lucrative grid contract always prompted him to pull out of baseball when the boys started kicking the football around early in the season. They say Parker would have been a magnificent diamond darling had he skipped football, for the bruising play of the latter sport took too much out of him physically.

Eric (The Red) Tipton made more of an effort to make the grade in the big leagues. He played an acceptable outfield for the Reds, then drifted back to the American Association. After Eric's departure, Lloyd Merriman came up and didn't exactly set the National Pastime on fire, though the Reds thought he had the stuff. Merriman was a guy who dropped football like a hot potato right in the middle of a successful pigskin career at Stanford.

Much is known of Branch Rickey's executive ability behind the big-league scenes. Little is remembered, on the other hand, of the fact that Branch was once a pretty brainy catcher although he consistently refused to play Sunday ball for the Cincinnati Reds or for anybody else. On top of this, back around the turn of the century Rickey blossomed forth as a gosh-darned good football player.

For appearing in the backfield of an Ohio professional eleven, Branch earned the stupendous sum of $150 per game. To draw that kind of money in those days, a pigskinner had to be exceptional at lugging the leather, and Rickey was. Exactly how far Rickey could have gone in pro football and whether baseball might have lost his genius was never determined because a broken bone in the leg brought a rapid end to Branch's backfielding.

You'd have to call infielder Johnny Berardino a versatile guy. Not long after Johnny departed the big leagues, he made the grade out in Hollywood with one of the big movie companies—and in front of the camera. Eventually, Johnny B. became an accomplished actor. A number of seasons back when the St. Louis Browns assigned Johnny to the Washington Senators, he aloofly announced that he was quitting the diamond game to enter the movies.

Quickly the Browns brought back Berardino to St. Louis. (This is an improvement?) Truthfully, the Browns believed every word of Berardino's about entering cinema city, for the classy infielder had been a child star on the silver screen. Nevertheless, the Brownies promptly erased dreams of Hollywood stardom from Johnny's mind by switching the second-sacker to the Cleveland Indians. The latter move was more to Berardino's liking, he no doubt deciding that the pay with a pennant contender was bound to be more consistent than that of a struggling movieland thespian.

Every Yankee fan has a soft spot in his heart for pitcher of yore, Charley Devens, the Harvard hotshot. The New Yorkers are probably the only team in history to have had on their roster at the same time a Harvard man—Devens—and a Yale man—Johnny Broaca. Those in the know claim that Charley Devens had talent plus, as well as the mental makeup to become a big-leaguer of elegance.

It seems though that Charley did not have to depend on baseball for a livelihood. Charley's family, had social standing in Boston and they wanted him to become a banker, which he did. As an athlete, though, young Devens had extraordinary ability. Harvard football followers will recall Charley Devens as one of the better grid guys to graduate from the Ivy League.

Eddie Dyer was in his younger days a dependable southpaw pitcher and in his later years a dependable manager for the St. Louis Cardinals. Eddie's abilities were not limited strictly to the baseball diamond, either. At Rice Institute, Eddie Dyer became one of the school's pigskin immortals. In 1921 he captained a great Rice eleven which has seen few equals in the Southwest. At that, Eddie was just as versatile in baseball. When he wasn't pitching, he played the outfield, for he could always level a lethal bat and he had speed to spare.

The list of famous football players who have switched to big-league baseball is large indeed. The dash and carry boys include such baseballers as Alvin (Blackie) Dark, Charley Dressen, Snuffy Stirnweiss, Christy Matthewson, and Mickey Cochrane, to mention a few. Howie Schultz, the long drink of infielder who covered first for the Dodgers during the latter war years, was a college basketball hero. Lou Boudreau, long-time Cleveland manager and American League ace shortstop, starred on the basketball court in college.

Most baseball players are versatile in the sense that they become successful businessmen during the off-season months. In more recent times, those two affluent Yankees Yogi Berra and Whitey Ford have exemplified the ballplayer turned businessman. Berra has been involved in bowling alleys and soft drinks. Ford, the all-time great lefty, did very well as a Wall Street customer's man, then went into business himself. Stan Musial is a successful restaurateur in St. Louis. A number of big leaguers have found employment as sports announcers after their baseball careers.

When you talk about versatile guys you certainly shouldn't overlook Abner Doubleday, founder of this sport of baseball, as is claimed in most quarters. Doubleday, a graduate of the United States Military Academy at West Point in 1842, won his medals under fire in three wars (the McCoy, not baseball ones). In the Mexican and Indian wars, old Ab made his mark as a marksman. As a captain of cavalry at Fort Sumter when the Civil War began, Doubleday fired the first Federal cannon in the war between the States. Decorated later at Gettysburg, Mr. Baseball was made a Major General and he is buried at Arlington National Cemetery, Arlington, Va. How he found time to invent baseball remains a mystery of proportions. As a matter of fact, in his Cadet days, Gen. Douglas Mac-Arthur was more than a passable outfielder for the West Point nine.

Everybody will remember Pepper Martin as the dashing, do-derring, daredevil third sacker of the St. Louis Cardinal Gas-House Gang. In spite of his size, Pepper had always been an acceptable football player, often joining up with the home-town youngsters just to play for the fun of it, for Pepper loved football.

It took Pepper a long time but he finally made national headlines as a pigskinner for the cash-and-carry pro leagues. The incident occurred in 1948 when Branch Rickey signed Martin to play for the Brooklyn Football Dodgers. Considered too old for a baseball game, Pepper was a prohibitive 40 for football competition when he reported. Rickey didn't expect Pepper to lug the leather, however; the Mahatma had signed Pepper as a place-kicker. Martin, though, didn't turn out to be a Ward Cuff so he soon sought employment elsewhere.

Pepper's career paralleled in a way that of Ken Strong. Though Ken's memory will always be cherished by New York Giant football fans, he still failed to make the grade as an outfielder for the Brooklyn Dodgers. Nevertheless, in semi-pro baseball Ken Strong had always been a standout covering the outer gardens for years with the Springfield Greys. Suddenly at 40, Ken Strong was back in the football spotlight when the Giants sent him a desperate plea to please do their place-kicking. Ken weighed the offer, accepted, and for a guy of 40 did right well for himself that season.

Charley Gelbert is remembered most as the pre-Marty Marion shortstop of the Cardinals who as a ball player was as solid as the rock of you know what until a hunting accident blasted his colorful career. Not so well remembered is the fact that Charley Gelbert made one of Walter Camp's famous All-American teams. At tiny Lebanon Valley College in Pennsylvania, the students and grads still speak of gridstar Gelbert as one of the greatest backfield men ever to lace on a pair of cleated shoes.

Gene Woodling, the distinguished American League veteran, had talent for more than bat and glove. Gene not only patrolled the outer pastures for Cleveland, the Yanks and the Mets, among others, but found time off the diamond to be an expert swimmer. Gene's got a box full of medals to prove his natatorial ability.

Former Dodger pitcher, Ralph Branca, was a good enough crooner to think of earning his living at it when his major league career was at an end. He did appear on several television shows and once made a vaudeville circuit tour. Teaming up with singing mates Carl Furillo and Eddie Miksis, Ralph cut a pretty good selling record and later the trio appeared on the well known Ed Sullivan "Toast of the Town" television show as a singing threesome.

Red Barrett, former St. Louis and Boston National League pitcher is a handy man with the voice. When the Braves were visiting NYC, Red starred on the Morey Amsterdam radio show, a program with a large local following at the time. Former first-sacker Buddy Hassett always boasted of a good set of pipes. Hardly a baseball meeting went by without Buddy raising his voice in a robust song.

Bob Lemon, the former Cleveland Indian great, achieved his greatest recognition as a right-handed pitcher. Yet, Lemon, even when at the height of his career still stubbornly insisted that he wanted to be an outfielder so he could play every day. Lemon, who came up to Cleveland as a third baseman in 1941, switched to pitching when he returned from the wars to the Tribe in 1946. In 1947 he was still leading a double life. As a pitcher he was 11-5 and as an out-fielder-pinch hitter, Lemon hit for a .321 mark. Don Newcombe, the former Dodger ace, was another pitcher who also was better than fair with the bat. In fact, big Newk was occasionally called on to pinch hit on some Dodger teams rich with sluggers. But the all-time mark for versatility still must go to the fabulous Babe Ruth. Few people realize what a great record the Babe made as a pitcher before he was turned into an everyday performer as an out-fielder. In fact, in the years 1916 and 1917, Ruth accounted for 47 mound victories as a member of the Boston Red Sox.

Handy Guys With Handicaps

On August 5, 1945, Bert Shepherd limped slightly to the mound of Griffith Stadium, Washington, from which vantage point he limited the opposition to three hits and one run over a 5⅓-inning span. In the course of his pitch hitch, Shepherd fanned two opposing batters.

Not an overwhelming performance, perhaps, but an adequate one and an even more impressive stint considering Bert Shepherd was pitching on one good leg. The other limb Shepherd lost in action during World War II. An aerial combat veteran, Bert suffered the crippling wound over Germany and skeptics said he would never again crank up his qualified left arm on a major-league baseball diamond.

Bert did okay for a while. However, operating off one good leg only proved too much of a handicap even for a stout-hearted individual like Shepherd. Fielding his position is as important to a pitcher as are his mound efforts and Bert just wasn't agile enough to dash in and scoop up those slow tricklers that twist along the foul lines. Others before Bert have tried to accomplish the same stupendous feat and have failed so the blow couldn't have been too severe when he failed to stick with the Senators in 1946.

There was also Monte Stratton of course. His big-league career from 1934 to 1937 had been an impressive one and after three full seasons in the big show he had definitely arrived, reached his pitching peak. Monte went hunting in 1938 and an accidental shot buried a bullet so deeply in his right leg doctors had to amputate. It looked like the end of a brilliant baseball career to everybody except Monty who got himself a wooden leg and tried a comeback. However, things like covering first base on a grounder to the right side and fielding a bunt efficiently just can't be done on a wooden leg so Monty accepted a position as a White Sox coach.

For some time Monty disappeared from the national baseball picture. The game, courageous guy didn't want coaching—he wanted pitching. Sometime in 1947 Monty's name again appeared in the nation's newspapers. Came the stimulating report that pitching for a minor-loop team, Monty Stratton had chalked up 18 solid victories, nothing to be sneezed at even for a guy with two good legs.

Pete Gray's first season with the Three Rivers Club in Quebec, Canada, will always be a subject of sports conversation north of the border. Pete had a slam-bangup year, leading the Canadian-American League with a .381 batting average. And Pete's feats weren't limited to stickout stickwork alone. He could field with the best of them, throw bullets with his left arm and sprint like a steer. On another occasion, Pete Gray had led the Southern Association in stolen bases for one season with 68. For that demonstration Pete earned the League's most-valuable player award.

Pete did all these things and yet he never made the grade in the majors. Why? Well, Peter Gray as you probably know had only one arm. The split second he lost in transferring his glove from his left hand to under what remained of his right arm so he could get the ball back to the infield just wasn't acceptable in the big play for pay.

In the American League his hitting for some reason fell off sharply and he was a bare shadow of the sensation he had been in the minors and in semi-pro ball. It's hard to believe, but when Pete swung the bat with one arm he generated almost as much power as many two-armed heavy hitters. Given two arms, Pete would no doubt have earned himself a permanent position in national pastime play.

The St. Louis Browns gave Pete his big chance at the end of World War II and though Gray flopped it wasn't for lack of trying. All his life Pete had played hard and with the Browns of 1945 he made no exception. Quite a few years have elapsed since Pete's last big-league appearance but few newcomers since have given it a harder hustle.

One of the best bargains in baseball is the buy that brought Charley Red Ruffing to the New York Yankees in 1930 in exchange for outfielder Cedric Durst and $50,000. During a productive big-league sojourn beginning in 1925, Ruffing notched more than 265 victories, stamping him as one of the all-time best. Yet Ruffing is, and always has been, slightly crippled.

At the age of 14 Ruff had four toes of his left foot sheared off in a soft-coal mine accident near his hometown, Nokomis, Illinois. Although he was still a kid, Red needed money badly for the family so he kept right at the job until he suffered another injury, this time to his right foot. The last mishap convinced young Charley Ruffing that there must be an easier way of earning a buck. He promptly switched to baseball. The success of his move is registered in the records. Yet his youth-time injuries had been so severe he saw only limited service in World War II, although he was inducted as an oldster of 38 in 1942.

Although pitcher Bobo Newsom arrived on this earth sound of body, baseball accomplished much in an attempt to break down the Great One's terrific torso. Bobo suffered as much injury during his career on the diamond as a day-dreaming lion tamer. In 1935 a line drive broke his kneecap. The very next season he was pitching for the Senators against the Yankees and Newsome had the misfortune to walk face first into a throw across the infield by third baseman Ossie Bluege.

Such a sock would fell most hardy men, most men that is except Bobo Newsom. Unbelievably, Bobo stuck to his guns and fired a 1-0 victory over the Yanks. After the game, doctors wired together his fractured jaw! Earlier in 1932 Newsom missed an entire National League season with the Cubs due to a leg fractured in his home before the campaign began. No sooner had unlucky Bob recovered from the accident than he got himself kicked by a mule and injured the same leg all over again.

Fainter hearts would have wilted under such punishment. Bobo Newsom, though, was never a quitter and in spite of such punishment he stayed with the game long enough to become one of baseball's oldest performers. Nobody really knew Bobo's age and very few could count the number of teams Bobo played with during his incredible big league career from 1929 to 1953.

When Mordecai Brown, the miner, as he was known, came up to the Browns in 1903, followers of the game snickered. "How could a guy with but three fingers on his pitching hand hope to control a baseball?" The criticism seemed logical, for Miner Brown had earlier lost two fingers of his pitching hand in a threshing machine accident. Yet Three-Fingered Brown went on to become one of the immortals of the pitching game, compiling an overall record surpassed by surprisingly few. Brown almost always earned 20 wins a season for the Cubs and one season he came up with a remarkable 29.

Loss of fingers meant no loss of durability to Mordecai. At one point during the 1908 stretch struggle with the Giants for the flag, Brown worked in 11 of 14 games and 14 of 19 games all told. In point of fact, this was the same year Brown won his 29 and with vital relief work tossed in he appeared in 43 winning ball games. Brown actually pitched the Cubs to a pennant in 1908.

The Three-Fingered flipper had a great Cub team behind him in 1908. The lineup included the famous Tinker to Evers to Chance infield. In the outfield were Solly Hofman in center flanked by Frankie Schulte and Jimmy Sheckard, all dependable players. Catcher Johnny Kling was the best in the business. Mordecai Brown headed the Cub pitching staff that held Detroit's miraculous Ty Cobb hitless in the last two games of the 1908 World Series as the Cubs walked off with the laurels.

About ten years after the turn of the century, a little second baseman, name of Miller Huggins was making baseball history. Nobody with the wildest imagination could claim Miller had the physical characteristics of a big-leaguer. Actually, little Miller tipped the scales at 140 and only after a heavy meal; still he was able to hold his own against those bone-crushing blocks hurled so commonly at second-sackers by sliding baserunners. Additionally, Huggins turned into one of the best leadoff men in the game for St. Louis. Always a battler, Huggins later became manager of the great Yankee block-busters of the Babe Ruth era and he brought his club three straight pennants in addition to other assorted wins.

Great little guys have always stood out in major-league play. Vic (Little) Lombardi measured no higher than the knee of a flea, but he was a consistent winner for the Dodgers around the time of World War II's end and Eddie Stanky, aggressive New York second-sacker, practically carried the Giants from the second division to third place in 1950 on his broad but low shoulders. Like Miller Huggins who managed to score 100 runs per season on three different campaigns, Eddie had a touted talent for getting on base. He almost always led his league in most bases on balls. Discounting Stanky's small stature, Dodger catcher Roy Campanella designated little Eddie as one of the National League's top 1950 hitters.

"He's hard to fool," opined catcher Campanella, "and he has a great batting eye. He'll foul off a dozen pitches to get a base on balls."

When you figure mites like Rabbit Maranville and

Wee Willie Keeler have made such remarkable base-ball history, you wonder why major-league moguls put such a premium on size in selecting team talent. Old timers still call Keeler the greatest hitter in his-tory—the hit 'em where they ain't champ of all time. Playing with the Baltimore Orioles of 1897, Wee Willie conspired with Jack Doyle to set a record never equalled to this day. Both Willie and Jack combined to slap out six base hits each out of six times at bat in the same game. Few batters since have duplicated the six-for-six feat and never on the same afternoon.

Bucky Harris is another of the little giants. Pretty much on the small side for an all-around athlete, Har-ris did not set Washington aglow when he reported as a rookie. What would the Senators want with another second-baseman when they had Maurice Shannon? "He was twice the ballplayer I was," Bucky later ad-mitted to sports writers. "But I ran him right out of the park." Bucky was another little man with gallons of guts. Small guys seem to be made up that way.

His spirit earned for Bucky Harris considerable fame. At 27 he became the Boy Wonder manager of the Senators and did such a jolting job he won the first pennant in history for the Capitol kids. Then Bucky went right out to top off a wonderful 1924 man-agerial debut by knocking off the Giants in four of seven games for a Series Victory.

Although Bucky was never a really good hitter, he was one of the best on the field. The D.P. combination of Roger Peckinpaugh and Bucky Harris was one reason the Senators sneaked the flag from the mur-derous Yankees. Another reason was rookie Goose

Goslin who latched onto that baseball for a neat .344 average and a league-leading 129 R.B.I.'s. Joe Judge, on first, was another ready reliable. What with the Bucky Harris zip and dash, though, it's small wonder the Nats won under the boy wonder.

The St. Louis Cardinals have had a couple of game guys covering third base during recent seasons. First of all there was staunch Whitey Kurowski, whose heart was as solid as his big bat. Two things Whitey definitely had—plenty of physical fortitude and plenty of courage. As a young boy Whitey fell off a fence into a pile of broken glass and gashed his throwing arm so severely the bone became infected and part rotted away. Kurowski though had such marvelous muscular tissue it held together the right arm between wrist and forearm through many major league campaigns although several inches of bone were actually missing.

In spite of this heartbreaking handicap, Whitey became one of the National League's number-one righthand power hitters during his lengthy tenure in the big show. When Whitey laid wood to baseball nobody could knock the apple any farther from the reaches of the ballpark.

A more recent Cardinal hot-corner custodian, Eddie Kazak, had part of his elbow shot away in combat during World War II. In spite of the severity of the wound and the placing of a plate in his arm, Eddie has never been found wanting in either department—fielding or hitting—and only the presence of brilliant Tommy Glaviano kept Kazak shuffling back and forth between bench and field.

The Cardinals, to be sure, can serve as a model to

the physical handicapped everywhere. The greatest of all recent Redbirds, Stan Musial, is the sort of guy who made his handicap pay off to advantage. Sometimes an injury changes a man's life for the better. It's like the blind man who sharpens his sense of touch and hearing to the extent that he becomes an accomplished musician.

Had it not been for an accident early in his career, Stan Musial might not have ranked with Ted Williams and Joe DiMaggio as one of the greatest batsmen of his era. Stan the Man, you see, wasn't always a solid socker.

As a matter of fact, Stan Musial's baseball career started on the pitching mound and he was a pretty promising hurler. One day he injured his meal-ticket—his left arm—and that was that. It looked like finis for a probable brilliant pitcher. Stan, though, is not easily discouraged. He quietly picked up an outfielder's glove and he's been chasing flies or covering first base ever since. No baseball fan needs refreshing on the hit history of Stan Musial. One may speculate, on the other hand, just how far Stan would have gone as a pitcher. By the widest stretch of the imagination, he could have been as good a pitcher as hitter, but certainly not better. As far as baseball is concerned, Stan's shoulder injury, painful as it probably was at the time, turned out to be nothing but a beautiful blessing.

As a paratrooper in Italy during the second World War Lou Brissie picked up enough enemy shrapnel to sink a frog. His entire body peppered with the deadly missiles, Lou suffered particularly damaging wounds in both legs. A promising major-league pitching career seemed certainly wiped out by the ravages of war.

The lanky, plucky lefthander joined the Philadelphia Athletics in 1947 with his leg in a brace. The chafing Lou experienced with every pitch caused blood poisoning to develop. Undaunted, Lou Brissie climbed from his hospital bed, went down to the minors and won 25 games that season. This was good enough to earn him another chance with Connie Mack's A's. Lou enjoyed a good season his freshman year and though his won and lost record after that was not impressive, his work on the mound was. He lost a lot of tough, low-score games in which the punchless Athletics failed to get him runs. Bad legs and all, he became the league's most effective lefthander.

One of the most outstanding outfielders ever to trot across the grass of an American League outfield was Joe DiMaggio. A big, strong guy in appearance and in fact, Joe suffered more than his share of injuries. With Joe, though, it was nothing but trouble every spring. Somehow or other he got hurt and throughout his star-studded career he invariably missed the season's opener with the Yanks.

In 1949 every expert counted Joe DiMaggio out and all washed up. The spur on his heel had become so painful Joe could scarcely lace on a baseball shoe. "This is the bitter end," predicted saddened baseball followers the world over. And it certainly seemed as if it were the end for Joe missed the entire first half of the 1949 season. Then Joe asked to play and if nobody in the nation thought he could, manager Casey

Stengel didn't share that opinion. He promptly inserted Joe DiMaggio in the lineup.

What Joe did from that point on is widely known. He picked up the Yankees and carried them to the pennant. Joe DiMag showed to particularly good advantage against the New Yorkers' toughest competitors, the Boston Red Sox. Line drives by DiMaggio knocked the paint off the fence at Fenway Park. Injury-hobbled, pain-wracked Joe DiMaggio never let a handicap handicap him. Even when that persistent spur burned holes in his heel he was out there slugging the apple and getting his share of base hits. Now of course Joe has retired from baseball and I doubt if there will ever be another like him.

"Go down to Richmond Hill High School, kid," the Giants and Dodgers both told Phil Rizzuto when he showed up for tryouts with these teams. The Yankees thought differently and put Rizzuto's name to a contract and they have never had cause to be sorry. Quite the contrary, for Phil the flea shone at Newark and became another little guy who cut a big path in the majors. Phil probably reached his heights in 1950 by batting well over .300 in helping the Yanks to the pennant and a four-straight Series sweep over the Phillies. As shortstop, Phil Rizzuto roamed like a hockey forward and grabbed everything within whistling distance. It came as a surprise to no one when pint-sized Phil Rizzuto of the Yanks earned the American League Most Valuable Player Award for 1950.

His former manager, Bucky Harris, probably paid Phil the greatest compliment when he said, "I wouldn't swap Rizzuto for any shortstop in baseball!

today." In addition to his fielding and hitting ability, Phil was always a master of the somewhat lost art of bunting. Very few of today's major-leaguers are adept at squeezing out a base hit via the bunt; in fact, many fail even to sacrifice a runner along at a crucial moment for want of bunting ability. Not so with Phil Rizzuto.

That Phil was a valuable 1950 Yankee was proved by his reported salary of $50,000 for 1951. That put him head and shoulders above all—(notwithstanding his scant stature)—in wages with the exception of Lou Boudreau. Not bad at all for a guy who measures no higher from the infield grass than five feet six inches. At that, Phil Rizzuto was probably one of the smallest guys to play varsity football in high school where he worked as quarterback for Richmond Hill.

The Yankees like the Cardinals seem to have had their share of handicapped stars. Lefty Gomez came to New York from San Francisco of the Pacific Coast League and when he reported he was 19 years old, stood six feet one inch high and weighed less than 160 pounds. The management figured they'd have to do something for this skinny southpaw so they fixed his teeth and fed him milk. That the diet succeeded is seen readily by a glance at Goofy's big-league pitching career. And he's just about the winningest guy ever to appear in the Major-League All-Star Game.

Steady But Unheralded

As a Giant, Lefty Al Smith was a flop, but hard. At length even shrewd Bill Terry, Giant skipper, gave up all hope and in 1937 cast the likeable lefty free. To all it looked like the end of the line for the southpaw after seven heart-breaking years in organized baseball.

Yet in 1945, Lefty Al Smith was still taking his turn on the hill for the Cleveland Indians and in an important game at Yankee Stadium he bluntly blanked the Bronx Bombers with five hits. At the time Al was 37 years old, an age when many big-league pitchers are retired to the farm picking up a soft buck pitching for the local semi-pro club on Sunday afternoon.

Al Smith was one of those steady, reliable players who rarely gain 72-point headlines but who performs capably, season after season, while the more heralded rookie sensations come and go. Like many a balanced ball player it took Al a little while to get going. Until he joined the Indians at 31 years of age, Al never really found himself. From that unbelievable point, however, he won 81 games in six years and by the time he whitewashed the Yanks in 1945, Al had chalked up 98 magnificent victories.

Consider the case of Wally Moses. A finer outfielder never picked up a glove. Wally will never rank with the Waners, the Wagners or the Wilsons, but on July 26, 1949, Wally Moses of the Athletics singled in the fifth inning of a game at Shibe Park to become the

86th player of the many thousands in the majors to attain the 2000-hit club. At the time speedy Wally was 38 years old and at 40 he was still up there taking his cuts.

It's hard to call Tony Lazzeri under-rated; yet his name is never mentioned in the same breath with such great second-sackers as Hornsby, Lejoie, Collins, Frisch, Gehringer, et al. Tony's greatest misfortune was paradoxically his greatest fortune—being a member of those New York powerhouses which included ball bashers like Ruth, Gehrig, Dickey, Meusel, and the rest. Although Tony wasn't a fielding flash, he was one of baseball's slickest second-sackers. He had power as his 60 home runs in the Pacific Coast League will bear out.

Unfortunately for Poosh-Em-Up Tony, he is remembered most as the man who struck out with the sacks soaked against old Pete Alexander in the World Series of 1926. It would be much kinder to picture the late keystone guardian as the Tony Lazzeri who became the second player in World Series history to strike a home run with the bases loaded, a feat he engineered in the 1936 Fall Classic, ten years after going down on strikes against Alexander. In the second game of the '36 Series, Lazzeri whacked five runs across the plate in addition to poling his grand slammer. The 18-4 score by which the Yanks downed the Giants marked the highest scoring contest in Series competition. And thanks to reliable, unsung Tony Lazzeri the Yankees were able to capture the 1936 Series honors from the Giants by a four-games-to-two margin.

When mentioning the great hitters of baseball, nobody would object to a list which included names like Jimmie Foxx, Joe Cronin, Mel Ott, Lloyd and Paul Waner. There isn't a guy among them whose name doesn't figure prominently in arguments about baseball's best batsmen. Here's another fellow to add to the list: Roger (Doc) Cramer.

Now Roger the Dodger is hardly ever mentioned as a stickout stickman. Yet this guy who stuck around Detroit as an outfielder almost as long as Henry Ford made motor chariots hardly gained the distinction due him. When Doc hammered out his 2,000 big-league base hit on June 10, 1942, he became one of the six active players at that time in both leagues to attain the goal. The other five banner batsmen were mentioned in the previous paragraph.

Reliable Roger came to bat 630 times in 1942, incidentally the eighth season in which he made more than 600 trips to the plate. Up to that time only two other players in major-league history, Sam Rice and Charley Gehringer, turned the 600-trip trick in eight seasons. What's more, Doc was always a better than average ballhawk. The six-foot, righty throwing, lefty batting fly-chaser from Manahawkin, N. J., was a hearty 36 when he joined the 2,000-hit club. In 1944, Cramer still going great, played in 144 games for the Tigers and compiled a .292 mark. By this time, indestructible Doc was 38. By 1946, Doc Cramer celebrated his 40th birthday and he did it in grand fashion, appearing in 68 games for the Tigers and hitting .294!

Take it from Chicago Cub or Brooklyn Dodger fans,

little Augie Galan was as good a ball player as you'll find anywhere, anytime in the majors. A steady outfielder, Augie was just as much at home on first base. And Augie could power that pill for a little guy. During his last few seasons with the wartime Dodgers, Augie was always right up there with the number-one hitters in the National League.

If you really want some idea as to Augie's ability to hit behind the base-runners—a difficult art—have a peep at his 1935 performance with the Cubs. That's the season which saw Galan play in 155 games without once hitting into a double play. For this ace accomplishment, Augie's name has gone down in the record books.

Traded to Cincinnati in 1947, Augie Galan nevertheless had batted a damaging .310 for his former team, the 1946 Dodgers. The California clouter had a .263 season with the Brooks in 1942 when they were overpowered by the Cards but in 1943 he upped this to .287 and in 1944 he again pushed up his batting percentage, this time to .318 in 151 games while slugging 94 runs across the plate. Born in 1912, Galan was 38 years old when he finished out his career in the big show with the Giants and Athletics of 1949.

When the steady Eddie pitchers of baseball are mentioned, Lee Meadows deserves a good, substantial plug if for no other reason than that he opened the gates to ball players operating under what baseball men thought at the time was a serious handicap. Meadows, you see, is the first ballplayer of record to wear glasses. Meadows came to the St. Louis Cards shortly before America's entry into World War I and sports writers, players and fans combined to look aghast at a pitcher with spectacles.

"It's downright suicide," was the gasp consensus. "He'll be killed—slashed and cut to ribbons." The only cutting, however, was done by Meadows as he cut opposing hitters down to his size. During his best single season, Specs Meadows packed away 22 victories and his over-all record is a standout. Both in 1925 and 1927, Meadows helped the Pirates to pennants. However, he was unable to gather himself a Series victory, dropping a game to Washington in 1925 and another to the Yanks in 1927.

Among the under-rated must be Earl Webb of the 1931 Red Sox. All Earl did that year was set a record for doubles in a season, drilling out 67 two-baggers. Joe Medwick, by the way, set the National League mark of 64 with the 1936 Cardinals.

Billy Goodman of the Boston Red Sox was one of those talented cookies who can play practically any position the game calls for. After holding down first for a couple of seasons with the Sox, Billy gave way to Walt Dropo and popped up in the lineup either at third or in the outfield. Because of his solid stickwork, Billy was a guy impossible to glue to the bench. Goodman's manager Steve O'Neil paid Billy the best possible compliment when he said, "He's the marvel of baseball."

Speak of standouts and you just can't overlook the smaller DiMaggio, another Red Soxer. Dom DiMaggio was a little guy with glasses who covered the outfield as slick and smooth as you've ever seen. Add to this the additional talents of a good arm and a keen batting eye and you're certain to have a ball-player who ranks with the finest in the business.

Brother Dom was another of those guys who has a real knack of getting on base. As a hitter, Dom lacked brother Joe's standout power, but he got more than his share of base hits. Crashing the big leagues with the Red Sox of 1940, Dominic DiMaggio hit a hearty .301. In six seasons with the Sox little Dom maintained a very nice .294 average. (He missed three war years.) His seasonal marks have been .283, .286, .316, .285, and .307.

"Dominic DiMaggio is a better player than his brother Joe!" That was a chant heard for years up Boston way.

In the eyes of Giant manager John McGraw, Bill Dahlen was one of baseball's most reliable performers. In McGraw's own words, Dahlen was the man who held together the Giants and led them to pennants in 1904 and 1905, the year they bested the Athletics in the World Series. Dahlen came to the Giants from Brooklyn where he had started at shortstop. McGraw gave Dahlen credit for developing young Arthur Devlin into one of baseball's most sparkling third-basemen.

"One of the greatest money players in the game," was the way McGraw always paid tribute to short-stop Bill Dahlen.

Bill DeLancey jumped from the minors to the St. Louis Cardinals in the early 1930's and he made an immediate hit with baseball's wise men everywhere. "Here is another Mickey Cochrane," they said with knowing nods, adding, "Perhaps better than Black Mike."

And DeLancey was good, superlative. He was smart; he could hit; he was agile as an adagio behind the plate and he had an arm of tempered steel. Bill caught the two Deans—Dizz and Paul—at their most fabulous heights. Then in 1936, disaster struck De-Lancey.

Bill the bright boy contracted a lung ailment, a blow that sent him straight to a sickbed. His condition failed to improve and there it was—finis for a career that was only beginning to blossom into the best. Bill DeLancey had to seek safety in the dry air of Arizona in 1936 and that was after only two brief seasons in the major leagues.

One of baseball's better relief pitchers has always been chunky Ted Wilks, talented bull-penner of the St. Louis Cardinals. And tough Ted has a mark he can point to with a good deal of satisfaction. During one stretch of his colorful career, Ted appeared on the mound in 80 consecutive ball games and was never charged with a loss. How many moundsmen can match such a mark?

Think of the great pitchers of baseball and you usually come up with such fellows as Walter Johnson, Christy Matthewson, Bob Feller, Dizzy Dean, or their likes. Yet there is still another who should gain himself a permanent position with baseball's mound immortals. He's Spud Chandler, ace of the New York Yankee mound staff until some years ago.

With the 1943 Yankees, Spurgeon Chandler won 20

games while dropping four, giving him the eye popping percentage of .833. That was enough to make
Spud the number-one pitcher of the majors. What's
more, Spud also led the majors in another department,
earned runs, by posting a sensational 1.64. His double
accomplishment gave Spud Chandler the honor of
becoming only the fourth hurler in American League
annals to achieve such a distinction. Other Junior
Circuit moundsmen to effect the difficult double were
Walter Johnson in 1913, 1914, 1918, and 1924; Lefty
Grove in 1929, 1930, 1931, and 1938 and Lefty Gomez
in 1934.

In speaking of under-rated players it is not possible
to skip the name of Vernon (Lefty) Gomez, teammate
of Spud Chandler. Like Chandler, as previously mentioned, Lefty was one of the only four American
League pitchers to lead his league in two depart-
ments during the same season—earned runs and percentages.

Granted, Lefty has had his share of fame but few
are aware of Lefty's outstanding World Series record.
Participating in four Fall Classics, Gomez has chalked
up six wins without a single setback! Consideration of
this feat shows the value of Lefty Gomez in its true
light.

Goofy Gomez was a member of the bone-crushing
Yankees who in 1932 crumbled the Cubs in four
straight games. Making one appearance in the Series,
Lefty Gomez pitched and won the second contest
5-2 while limiting the Chicago gang to nine hits.

Back again in World Series play in 1936 Gomez

took advantage of some heavy hitting on the part of his Yank teammates to gain two wins over the New York Giants. In the second game of the Series lucky Lefty found himself with a 9-1 lead at the end of three innings and he breezed through to an 18-4 win over the New York rivals permitting them but six hits. For the Giants, Schumacher, Smith, Coffman, Gabler and Gumbert all took it on the chin as the Yanks rolled up that biggest score in Series history.

It took a seven run rally in the top of the ninth in the sixth and final game plus help from fireman John Murphy, but Lefty again got his victory, this time by a 13-5 count. There can be little doubt that Gomez was the recipient of some of the heaviest hitting in World Series history in grabbing his pair of 1937 wins as the Yanks took the Giants six games to two.

In 1937, Lefty Gomez once more assumed the position on the mound as a member of the pennant-winning New Yorkers. The honor of opening the Series and closing the Series fell to Vernon Gomez. In the initial contest he tamed the same rivals as the year previously, the Giants, by an 8-1 score, holding the visitors to six scattered base knocks. By topping the Giants again in the fifth game, 4-2, while permitting eight safeties, Lefty locked up the Classic for the Yankees four games to one. As in 1936, Lefty benefited by some solid slugging in the first game when his mates hopped on Carl Hubbell for seven runs in the bottom of the sixth to sew up the contest. However, as far as Lefty Gomez is concerned, he probably earned his biggest thrill as a batter in that fateful bottom of the sixth. Lefty who loved to bat though he couldn't hit walls in a house walked twice in that sixth inning!

Came the World Series of 1938 and with it the last of Lefty Gomez in Autumn competition. Duplicating the devastating job of their 1932 brothers, the New York Yankees steam-rollered over the unlucky Cubs of Chicago in four straight tilts. As a result the Cubs went zero-for-eight in two straight World Series!

In the second game Lefty wrote his Swan Song as a World Series competitor and he did it in style, vanquishing the Cubs 6-3. In this one, the poor Cubs outsticked the Yanks by 11 to 7 but Yankee power brought home the bacon. Likeable Lefty wasn't around at the finish, so Fordham Fireman Johnny Murphy had to give El Goofo an assist in wrapping up the latter's sixth straight World Series victory without a setback.

More than a half-dozen times, the name of Ken Keltner has appeared in All-Star Game lineups and before being dropped by the Red Sox in 1950, Ken was a sprightly 34-year-old big-league performer. In firm figures, Ken the Kelt stuck around the majors for 12 long seasons and rated as the choice hot-corner custodian of the American League for most of them.

A real solid socker, Ken Keltner has always been a dangerous long-ball hitter. Still a green performer in 1939, clouting Keltner whistled three consecutive home runs out of Fenway Park against the Boston Red Sox. While his batting mark of something less than .300 spoke well for Ken Keltner, he sparkled on the field like a diamond on a diamond. Sports writers have always remarked most, perhaps, about the ability of Ken Keltner to backhand smashes down the third-base-line. They say he did this better than anybody in baseball.

Among the most underrated players, former Dodger Carl Furillo deserves special mention. "Peg O' My Heart" was the way former Brooklyn Dodger manager Burt Shotton used to refer to Carl because of his rifle arm, rated by many as one of the finest ever to be seen in baseball. Carl added brains to his brawn as well and was annually one of the leaders in assists among outfielders and played the right field wall at the Dodgers old home, Ebbets Field, as if he built it.

Furthermore, Furillo developed into a menacing hitter. With a career average of just about .300, Carl almost single-handedly led the Dodgers to the pennant in 1949 when he picked up where Jackie Robinson suddenly left off and slam-banged the Brooks into first place. Carl was a real streak hitter and when he was on a tear, opposing pitchers really had to duck for cover.

The 29-year-old Reading (Pa.) Rock had trouble breaking into the regular Dodger lineup. Both Leo Durocher and Burt Shotton were of the opinion that Carl couldn't hit a good curve-balling right-hander. Then Carl got mad and put these theories to pot by belting over .300 in 1949 and 1950 against all types of pitching. For Brooklyn, Carl Furillo was a bargain and then some. They got the Reading Rock along with the entire Reading franchise for a pithy $1,500.

Certainly among the most reliable of right-hand baseball pitchers has been Larry Jansen of the New

York Giants. Larry had one big quality missing from most major league moundsmen these days, the quality of control. With Jansen a walk was about as rare as a laughing umpire.

Stan Musial, who faced Jansen for years, confessed that Larry was one of his toughest mound foes. His manager, Leo Durocher, considered Jansen one of the top men he's ever managed, a guy with lots of heart. And with Leo, heart is all-important.

As in the case of many control pitchers, Jansen has an annoying habit of dishing up home-run balls. This is contrasted with the few usually hit off the fast, wild boys who keep a batter both on his toes and plenty loose up there at the plate.

In his 30th year, Larry enjoyed one of his best seasons with the Giants, the campaign of 1950. Fourth in the Senior Circuit among the low-earned-run-average experts, Larry probably turned in his greatest major-league accomplishment in the All-Star Game by holding the American Leagues at bay and scoreless until his mates could get him the lone run he needed for one of those rare National League triumphs.

It took a 30-win season at San Francisco in the Pacific Coast League back in 1946 to earn Jansen his chance with the Giants in 1947. Unlike many minor-league pitching prodigies, silent Larry carried his ability up to the majors where he posted a remarkable 21-5 record during his first season. He rounded out that year's chore with a nice 3.16 earned run average.

In the books of both his big league managers, Mel Ott and Leo Durocher, Larry Jansen was a genuine major-leaguer, a hard worker with plenty of savvy and plenty of raw courage.

When Pete Suder was covering second-base for the Philadelphia Athletics, his teammates pointed him out as baseball's most under-rated performer. "Pete Suder is the deftest fielding second-sacker in baseball," claimed Pete's buddies in chorus.

That the A's may have had something there is borne out by the facts. As a double-play executor, Pete is not excelled. During the 1948 season, Suder teamed up with shortstop Eddie Joost to rattle off 180 twin-killings, a high mark in almost any man's league. Defensively, Pete was just about tops, committing hardly any errors of any kind.

"You can't say too much about Pete. He's a real ball player in every respect." The testimonial came from shortstop Joost.

Pete Suder unfortunately was always dogged because of a comparatively light stick. A strapping six-footer—although he seemed smaller—Pete nonetheless was a heavy hitter in the spring. But as the season wore on his batting average would droop. Many pitchers, however, were careful with him, for Suder was a dangerous man in the clutch.

Pete Suder's big ambition was to hit .300, but he never made it in the majors, finishing his career with a none too robust .249 lifetime average.

Under New Management

The turnover among baseball managers is more than a little akin to the arrival and departure of lawmakers in the Congress of the United States. With the exception of Connie Mack, few field leaders stick it out for any great length of time with the same team though most bounce back from time to time to assume direction of another ball club.

The average baseball manager could be put in the same class with a bigamist—he just has too many people to please and it can't be done. The manager who can strike perfect harmony with the ballplayers, the club owners, the press, and the fans has just never been invented. Put yourself in the place of any baseball manager and figure how long you would last on your particular job if every move you made was watched by hundreds of thousands and if every error you made was blared out in nice juicy headlines.

The managerial genius of today is the flop of tomorrow and vice-versa. When Casey Stengel tried to right the upside-down Dodgers and Braves he was looked upon as a clown without a good deal of talent. As leader of the Yankee pennant winners of 1949 and 1950, Ole Case earned applause as the shrewdest of all. With the Yankees, Joe McCarthy was considered somewhat of a big baseball mind. In Boston, Red Sox rooters shouted for his scalp.

That's the way it has always been and that's the way it will always be. When you consider a long-time favorite son like Mel Ott couldn't stick with the Giants, then nobody can make good over an extended period. In three seasons as Dodger bench boss, Burt Shotton won two pennants and missed another on the last day of the season which certainly is par for the course. How then can you figure the Brooklyn bosses dropping Burt for incompetence? You can't. Eddie Dyer of the Cards was always in the thick of the pennant fight but when his team sagged in 1950 for the first time in years he was put at leisure. A more able manager than Eddie Dyer you won't find anywhere.

One of baseball's better-liked gentlemen is Billy Southworth, skipper of the Boston Braves; yet turbulence has marked the career of this diamond strategist. Fresh in public minds is the lack of courtesy extended him by his Braves of 1949 who went so far as to vote Billy out of first-division money although the ballot was ultimately changed.

Fewer folks remember back to 1929 when a younger Billy Southworth had a running headache trying to manage a band of rough and ready Cardinals. Taking over the reins from Bill McKechnie, Billy the Kid soon found himself in hot water with players who apparently resented nothing more than his youth. In an effort to enforce discipline, the Card pilot threatened fines for any behavior which he considered out of line. Mutiny resulted. As a result, Southworth's first fling at managing in the majors was an unhappy one and of necessity a short-lived one.

Serving with the 1933 Giants as a spring-training

coach, Billy Southworth is said to have traded punches with his boss, manager Bill Terry. Whether or not the story is true hasn't been proved, but when the season opened, Billy was no longer on the Giant coaching lines. Since that time, skipper Southworth has enjoyed a more peaceful time of it in the big show except for that one season, the year of 1949, Boston A.D.

Writing for Jack Schwartz's excellent Giant fan magazine some years ago, top announcer Ernie Harwell described one of baseball's most superstitious men—George Stallings, manager of the Miracle Braves of 1914. Surely you recall stories of Boston's minute-men of the hour, the team that jumped from last place in mid-season to the pennant, going on to sweep the strong Athletics in four straight for the World Series championship? Stallings, by the way, had such a wonderful defensive nine in 1914 the Beantowners were able to hold the Mackmen to an anemic .172 batting average in the annual autumn classic.

Getting back to Harwell on Stallings, Ernie points out how on the day the Braves started their fabulous comeback surge from the National League's cellar, Stallings was forced to park his car some three blocks from the field. Each day until the end of the season he continued to leave the jalopy three blocks away no matter how many empty spaces were closer.

During the start of one Brave rally, Stallings stopped to tie his shoe-lace. Then while ten Boston runs crossed the plate in a long drawn-out inning, Stallings remained in his cramped position for fear of breaking the spell. Stallings actually had to be carried to the clubhouse where a trainer took the knots out of his muscles.

The pet peeve of manager Stallings was always directed against any scrap of paper in front of the Boston dugout. So great was his peeve, George instructed the batboy to keep the area free of any paper no matter how tiny.

It didn't take the fans of Philadelphia long to get on to Stallings' abhorrence for paper, so one fine afternoon they conspired to tear up paper and toss it over the Brave dugout practically to the feet of the infuriated manager. Stallings, though, was not so easily hexed. During the next Boston-Philadelphia series in the Quaker City, George put his cash on the line and bought out every seat near his dugout!

It shouldn't take you more than one guess to name the youngest manager in the history of baseball. That's right, it was Lou Boudreau who took over at the helm of the Cleveland Indians in 1942 when Louie was a baseball baby of 24. Alva Bradley's faith in the youngster paid off as Boudreau always had his Injuns in the thick of the fight.

Then along came Bill Veeck to control the Cleveland club and insiders whispered that Lou was a sure thing to go. Jimmy Dykes or Charlie Grimm would certainly be appointed to succeed Boudreau, they said, but Lou lingered on. Hank Greenberg at length put an end to the star shortstop's tenure with Cleveland by peddling Lou to the Boston Red Sox during the winter of 1950. Greenberg, therefore, succeeded where Veeck failed.

As far back as 1947, Bill Veeck hinted that Lou

might leave Cleveland, announcing that he had all but put the finishing touches to a Brown-Indian swap of shortstops, Vern Stephens for Lou Boudreau. The story broke in many of the major newspapers and Veeck ran for cover. Always a well-liked guy in Cleveland, Lou Boudreau had something like 25,000 supporters who wrote to Veeck and threatened mayhem if the owner traded the manager-shortstop. As a result, Lou Boudreau remained in Cleveland.

Luckily for Veeck he didn't trade Lou, for the swatting shortstop bounced back the very next season, 1948, to lead his league in hitting with a .355 average and his dash and hustle finally brought a pennant to Cleveland. The Boudreau incident brings forth the observation that sometimes the average fan knows much more about baseball than he receives credit for.

Although Lou Boudreau had a rather rocky time of it with the press when he first took over the Indians, he seemed to improve his relations with the newspaper gents as seasons rolled by. After the kid manager learned he could no more dictate to the papers than he could tell the fans how to root, he straightened himself out in the matter of public relations.

Aside from the reputation of baseball clown Casey Stengel built as manager of the hapless Dodgers and Braves during the dark days of the second division, he also made his mark as something of a Giant killer. It was Casey's daffy Dodgers, you see, who knocked Bill Terry's classy clique right out of the pennant during the last two games of the 1934 season and the Dodgers did it right in the ballpark of the hated over-the-river rivals, in the Polo Grounds.

It was in 1934 that Bill Terry, riding high with his Giants, got off the infamous and back-firing barb, "Is Brooklyn still in the league?" Imagine the chagrin of Giant followers everywhere when the Brooks proved they were in the league by snatching the precious pennant from the New Yorkers!

In the dying days of 1934, the Giants and Cardinals were battling neck and neck for the prized bunting. While the Cards were struggling at home with Cincinnati, New York was entertaining the floundering flock of Stengel at the Polo Grounds for a two-game setto. At the start of the Giant-Brook series the St. Louis club and the New York club were in a flat-footed tie for first place.

As Brooklyn astounded the baseball world by slapping the Giants, the Cards took their game from the Reds and moved into undisputed position of first place. On the season's finale, St. Louis again edged Cincinnati while the remarkable Flatbush nine was pinning back the ears of Terry's terrors. Thus the Cards copped the title and Casey Stengel quietly asked, "Is Brooklyn still in the league."

Another Stengel claim to fame is the pickoff play worked so neatly by the pennant-winning Indians of 1948, only with Casey it was labelled the precision play. The only trouble with Casey's precision play was that the 1930's Dodgers lacked precision.

As with Boudreau's pickoff in Case's case, the shortstop would sneak to second and the catcher would signal the pitcher to count three and whirl while throwing. In spite of such neat plans, the daffy Dodgers rarely caught a runner off second base.

The precision play failing, persistent Case came up with a freeze play. The pitcher had his instructions to throw the ball at the batter's head while shouting a warning. Naturally, the hitter would hit the dirt giving the catcher a surefire clear throw to third where a base-runner was to be picked off. Casey figured the runner would take his lead and freeze as he heard the warning shout from the pitcher and saw his teammate drop to the ground.

Casey's freeze play failed because of one glaring flaw. Not only would the runner leading off third freeze but the Dodger third-baseman would invariably freeze along with him. The result was an errant peg into left-field by the catcher allowing the runner to score easily from third.

Before Eddie (Muggsy) Stanky joined the Giants, the New Yorkers had another Muggsy. He was John J. (Muggsy) McGraw and he made an untouchable reputation at Coogan's Bluff by bringing ten pennants to the flagpole of the Polo Grounds, four buntings in a row from 1921 to 1924.

In spite of McGraw's ability to cop pennants he was not so successful in World Series play. His Giants grabbed Series laurels three times, losing six times, there being no contest in 1904. Although John earned three straight flags in 1911-12-13, he nonetheless dropped the World Series three times in a row, twice to the Athletics and once to the Red Sox.

Perhaps the most disappointing team of all time for McGraw was the New York contingent of 1925. From 1921 to 1924 the jarring Giants had reigned supreme over the National League. Four times they had grabbed the pennant. Muggsy McGraw had visions of five straight flags and a record most difficult for any manager to match.

The McGraw team of 1925 was basically the same at the start, only a little older, and, as events proved, a little too old. Still from April until June the Giants led the National League pack and McGraw was trotting on air. Enter the villains—the Pirates. The bold Bucs took over first place and maintained their wicked pace until the first of August when McGraw whipped his New Yorkers back into the lead.

It was nip and tuck until John's veterans began to stagger. Heinie Groh at third base handed over his glove to newcomer Freddie Lindstrom while Emil Meusel and Ross Youngs sagged in the outfield. Despite the fact that Billy Southworth, Louis Wilson and Frank Walker helped bolster the outer garden and Frank Snyder carried on capably behind the plate, McGraw could no longer get necessary mileage out of his pitchers.

No longer was Hughie McQuillan the invincible moundsman as he won a measly two games while dropping a trio. Portsider Artie Nehf showed an unimpressive 11-9 record, the same as Jack Bentley. Other disappointing marks were the 15-11 of Virgil Barnes and the 14-15 of John Scott. All in all the Giants of 1925 were on the downgrade and with themselves they dragged their scrapping pilot, John McGraw.

Uncle Wilbert Robinson was the Brooklyn Dodger manager noted for his good humor and for his ability to squeeze good seasons out of ballplayers well past their primes. That Uncle Robbie had his Dodgers in the thick of pennant fights as often as he did is tribute plenty to the diamond mastermind as his Brooks at best were usually a collection of clowns.

For most of Robinson's life he had been a close pal of John McGraw's. Then when Robbie jumped his job of coach under Muggsy McGraw to manage Brooklyn, friendship developed into one of the most violent hates ever witnessed in the national pastime. The ballyhooed Brooklyn-New York feud became stunning reality with McGraw piloting the Giants and Robbie guiding the Dodgers.

Whipping the Giants of McGraw always gave Uncle Robbie loads of satisfaction and it was to his disadvantage that Brooklyn didn't accomplish the trick more often. Yet, in spite of the oft low position in league standings of the Brooklyn bums, they always rose to the heights against New York to play like demons and keep the intra-city series rivalry at a pretty close level in percentages.

Many are the baseball minds who refuse to manage a major-league team for love or money due to the high mortality rate among bench masterminds. For that very reason Arthur Fletcher steadfastly refused to listen to offers offering him the opportunity of managing a big-league nine. Arthur much preferred to serve as Joe McCarthy's lieutenant, drawing a steady salary for coaching year after year without growing grey hairs, worrying over the attitudes of fans, sports writers and club owners.

Like Fletcher, Tommy Henrich and Jim Turner, later day Yankees, declined managerial positions to remain in the New York organization as coaches. Former top twirler in the majors, Milkman Jim Turner, definitely refused a position as field general of the St. Louis Cardinals, an assignment looked upon by many as one of the most choice in baseball. It's also said the Dodgers of 1950-51 made a pitch for Henrich before signing popular Chuck Dressen. What's more, Tommy additionally turned down a minor-league offer to pilot the Kansas City Blues. The Cardinals and A's also sent out feelers to Henrich, all to no avail.

Some managers prefer a happy position in the minors to a harassing one in the majors. A good example is Lefty O'Doul, longtime skipper of the PCL San Francisco Seals. Lefty turned out top teams on the Coast for years and became a prolific developer of major league talent. About half of the franchises in the majors tried to woo Lefty, but he wouldn't succumb to all their blandishments for he knew all too well the pitfalls of the job.

Dean of all major-league managers has always been of course Connie Mack, for 50 years the leader of the Philadelphia Athletics. Connie had his ups and downs like everybody else; still his baseball brilliance sparkled more often than not. Tragic indeed is the fact that Connie had to retire from his popular position at the close of 1950 under fire because of the fate of his last place A's. Unfortunately for Connie, most of baseball's experts picked his club to do better so the blame fell directly on his narrow but still straight shoulders. Not seeing Mr. Mack direct his ball club from the Philadelphia dugout by means of a nervous scorecard struck a solemn note for many an Athletic fan.

In his better days, Connie Mack guided some of the strongest ball clubs ever to appear on a diamond. His Athletics of 1911 and 1913, as previously recounted, knocked off the jet-propelled Giants of McGraw twice in World Series play. His pennant-winning A's of 1929, 1930 and 1931 were so tremendous Connie finally broke up the team to maintain a measure of balance in the American League. Those same A's smothered the Cubs in the 1929 World Series four games to one, jolted the Cards in the 1930 Series four games to two and lost to the same underdog Cards in 1931 four games to three.

It is debatable indeed whether any team in the history of baseball boasted more genuine talent than Connie Mack's Philadelphia fellows of the 1929 era.

On that club Connie had such stellar stars as the great Jimmy Foxx, Lefty Grove, George Earnshaw, Rube Waddell (a trio of pitchers par excellence), Al Simmons, Mickey Cochrane and Jimmy Dykes. Then there was another still effective pitcher, Waite Hoyt. Can any of today's teams even approach such a collection of all-stars?

Many honors have been bestowed on the venerable gentleman of baseball management. One was the berth as field director of the first American League All Star team in 1933. For a rival, Connie drew John McGraw as pilot of the National Leaguers. Mr. Mack showed to splendid advantage as his team walloped McGraw's 4-2 in Comiskey Park, Chicago. Big man of the day was, of course, Babe Ruth who provided the victory margin in the third inning when he found Charley Gehringer on base and belted a two-run homer out of the park. At the time, the Bambino was 38 years old but his bat still packed plenty of punch.

In 1948 aged Connie had his last chance for a stab at glory. Almost everybody was pulling for Mr. Mack's A's to make the grade so Connie could wind up a lengthy career in real style. And the Philadelphia Athletics almost pulled the upset of the decade by grabbing the American League flag for Connie. During the first half of the season, the Mackmen were right up there slugging it out with the Yankees, Red Sox and Indians. As late as August the A's were still in a veritable four-team tie for first place until Connie's kids suffered a crippling blow, an injury to shortstop Eddie Joost. As the talented veteran was just about Philadelphia's most valuable player, the Athletics never could overcome his loss so Connie had to settle for place money in his last all-out bid for a pennant before retiring.

Most explosive manager on major league record has been without doubt Lippy Leo Durocher. By his own admission, Durocher is a guy who plays with his heart on his sleeve, a guy who hates to lose no matter what the circumstances and a guy who will go to any lengths to win. In spite of Leo's irksome field tactics, he is oddly enough usually well-liked by his ball players.

When Leo suddenly left the Dodgers to take over as manager of the Giants most of his hired help came forth and expressed genuine concern over seeing Leo leave. Only exception to the loyalty rule has been Eddie Stanky who was swapped from Durocher's Dodgers to the Boston Braves and who commented, "I've been knifed in the back." Still, Eddie came back to work under Leo at the Polo Grounds and the two hit it off as well as in the old days.

As tough as Leo has always been with the opposition and with umpires, he has been a virtual father to young rookies on his club. Always a soft touch, Durocher has handed out money freely to low-salaried kids without every trying to collect. And if any of Leo's players ever get in trouble, the fiery pilot will plunge right into the fight.

As a Cardinal shortstop back in the days before he assumed the managership of the Dodgers Leo had a run-in with the then Brook pilot, Casey Stengel. Without batting an eyelash, Lippy Leo invited Casey under the stands to have it out. Just as quickly, Stengel accepted.

"He hit me with a bat," Durocher always protested in describing the fracas.

"Bat my eye," replied Stengel. "It was my fist. Leo thought it was a bat."

Amateur statisticians figure quick-tempered Durocher has paid at least $2,000 in fines for conduct unbecoming a ball player. Among others he has squared off against are such solid thumpers as Ted Meier, Associated Press sports writer, Dick Bartell, Mickey Owen and Zeke Bonura. Meier always insisted Leo hit him when he wasn't looking.

Umpires and Durocher have as all know never been bosom buddies. At one time or another, Leo has tangled with just about every man in blue. Every time you have seen Durocher tossed out of a game it usually has been because of the manager's uncontrollable and ungentlemanly language.

Particular target of the Lippy one had always been big George Magerkurth. Durocher would allow hardly a game to pass without saluting Mage from the dugout by calling him a good loud "meat-head." The word is said to have set big George on fire.

Joining the Yanks of 1928 as a fresh-kid shortstop, Leo Durocher soon earned his title of "Lip." One of Leo's first big-league acts was to give hard-charging, reckless Ty Cobb the hip. This action endeared Durocher to Babe Ruth although the pair had been bitter enemies from the very outset.

Ruth had baptized Durocher the "All-American Out" while Leo had called Ruth nothing but a guy with lots of brawn and little brains.

The chief reason Durocher didn't stick longer than a couple of seasons with the Yankees was his love for high living. Even in later life he fraternized with the Broadway-Hollywood sophisticates but as a young shortstop in 1930 he could afford no such luxuries. Deep in debt, Leo's play fell off and he at length was waived to the Cincinnati Reds.

As a sort of bonus for a promise to be good, the Reds paid off Durocher's creditors and got the sprightly shortstop rolling to the extent he soon became the National League's number-one man at his position. With the Cardinals, later, he soon found himself in pennant play. Never a really fine hitter, Leo was a tremendous hustler, a sparkling shortstop and an adequate enough stickman in the clutch.

One of the most unique character combinations in baseball was the Larry MacPhail-Leo Durocher alliance at Brooklyn in 1939. Not completely sold on Durocher at the outset, laughing Larry nevertheless was impressed by his new manager's dash and drive. The faith of MacPhail was justified for Durocher brought the Dodgers in third—with only one .300 hitter—the highest standing for the Flock of Flatbush in years.

In eight seasons with the Dodgers, Durocher did not set the league on fire. His Dodgers captured but a single pennant, winning one and losing four in World Series play. His 1942 Brooklyn team blew a late-season ten-game lead to the Cardinals. Durocher's dandies finished second three times, third three times and seventh once. At that, he did manage to spend most of his time in the fast company of the first division, though.

Men In Boo

Baseball umpires are usually described as the men in blue, though men in boo would be more appropriate after weighing their popularity with the fans—or unpopularity to be more honest. Many times the cry "Kill the Ump" has echoed through an American ball park, but the job appears not so easy. Umpires as a group are just about as indestructible as you-know-what rock. Earning a living by standing behind the catcher and frequently feeling the full impact of a foul tip toughens a man as does nothing else. Consequently, most umpires are big boys fully capable of holding their own in any altercation.

One of the roughest, toughest umps to don mask and chest-protector has been 230-pound George Magerkurth, every ounce a man. Most of George's troubles were always Dodgers. His most rousing run-in with the Flatbush Flock occurred on an afternoon in Philadelphia some seasons back when big George chased no less than the entire Brooklyn bench to the clubhouse leaving on the field the minimum number of players to complete the game.

Everything started in the usual Durocher-Dodger pattern of the time. First, Eddie Stanky squawked loud and long over a third strike. No sooner was excitable Eddie en route to an early shower, than Leo Durocher took up the cudgels and he too headed for a premature bath. At the point where the entire

Dodger dugout took to heckling Mage, the infuriated official gave them all the heave-ho.

Mr. Magerkurth has always been a sort of thorn in the Brooklyn side. One Flatbush fan became so irate after a close decision against his darling Dodgers during the crucial 1940 pennant fight, he jumped George immediately after the last out of the afternoon and had the angry arbitrator flat on his back and helpless. Big George, more bewildered than hurt, didn't have a chance to fight back. Even Larry MacPhail, the Brooklyn majordomo, campaigned to have the honest ump banished from the league, but he failed of course.

Only one season earlier, the same George Magerkurth had a peck of trouble on the other side of the river where he clashed with the New York Giants. Friction reached such a pitch at the Polo Grounds that the "Stree-ike" man finally came to blows with Giant shortstop Billy Jurges. Like all men in blue or boo, Magerkurth, however, rarely lost a battle and never an argument.

When Bill Klem retired from active umping duty in 1941 to assume directorship of all umpires, a little something went out of baseball. At the time Bill was a healthy 67 and time did not diminish the volume of his voice. Let Bill toss a player out of the ball park or call a strike and you could hear the decision to the far corners of the most distant stands.

Bill Klem was famous for drawing a spiked line with his foot across the path of an enraged ball player. Cross that line and the player was through for the day and most knew and respected the border line. Because of his inherent insistence on discipline, Klem himself drew punishment of a nature probably never before or after administered to an umpire. For accosting outfielder Goose Goslin off the field and laying down the law about conduct on the diamond, Bill earned a $50 fine and the brushoff in every World Series assignment from 1934 on.

"The $50 is for using abusive language to a ball player," was the startling explanation of Judge Landis.

Bill Klem called only two real wrong ones in his career—at least two that were reversed. One took place long ago in 1911 and concerned Honus Wagner who showed his contempt for a base on balls by stepping across home plate as if to hit at every errant pitch. Four such wide pitches sailed by and Klem motioned Wagner to first base.

Immediately Cincinnati manager Clark Griffith stormed the stormy Klem but Bill stood by his decision and drew with his toe the famous battle line. A couple of days later Bill was shocked to learn he was overruled and that Wagner was automatically out for leaving the batter's box.

Exactly 23 years went by before Bill called another wrongo. This decision he rendered in 1934 with Chuck Klein hitting for the Cubs against St. Louis with the bags loaded. Chuck popped high in the air and the Red Bird catcher permitted the ball to drop safely. "Fair ball!" roared Klem as Klein sprinted for first and made it safely. Meanwhile the run scored prompting the Cards to charge Klem like a herd of wild geese. "Klein is out," they screamed, "infield fly!"

"Infield fly my eye," insisted Klem. "Is the catcher an infielder?"

Nevertheless, the National League president agreed with the Cardinals and eventually overruled Klem's decree.

As with all other umpires, the genuine honesty of Bill Klem could never be questioned in the slightest. One of the umpires officiating at the important, memorable Cub-Giant playoff game of 1908 to decide the pennant in favor of the Cubs was none other than able Bill Klem. Fever ran so high that Dr. William Creamer, a sort of off-the-record physician for the Giants, is reported to have thrust a flock of greenbacks into the hand of Klem in an alleged attempt to sway that important personage's judgment on the field next day. Klem, of course, would have none of that and Dr. Creamer found himself barred from any baseball participation for the rest of his life.

Nobody can talk umpires without mentioning Billy Evans who saw service in the big show for a couple of decades during the great days of Ty Cobb, Babe Ruth, Walter Johnson and other greats. Like every other umpire, Evans had his run-ins with the players. However, his biggest tormenter seemed to be Ty Cobb.

Billy and Ty are reported to have ultimately decided to "settle it under the stands." The Georgia peach knocked the arbiter cold but the old ump always maintained that Cobb took unfair advantage of him and butted him before Billy was able to put up his fists.

At any rate, Billy Evans easily survived the cranium kayo and came back in later years as vice-president of the Detroit Tigers.

The invention of the improved camera to newspaper coverage of the national pastime has made the
umpire's job an even more discouraging one. A blun-
der by the man in blue is not so easily overlooked with
the newspaper photographers and their high-powered
lenses right on top of every play and with the close-up
television cameras in the same position. Often the
home T.V. viewer—one of hundreds of thousands perhaps—is in a much better position to call a play than
is the man on the actual playing field.

On several occasions newspaper pictures have ex-
posed wrongos called by unhappy umpires, most notable, perhaps, occurring during the World Series between Cleveland and Boston in 1948. Early in the
Series, the Indians tried their famed pick-off play with
the pitcher counting and whirling blindly to second
base. It appeared to almost everybody looking on, except umpire Bill Stewart, that the Clevelanders successfully picked Brave catcher Phil Masi off base.
This was a crucial decision for Masi eventually went
on to score the game's only run in a 1-0 Boston victory.
The very next day practically every newspaper in
the country carried a closeup picture of the play and
to all eyes, Masi was quite definitely out. Had the
play been called differently, the game's outcome
might have been otherwise. However, league officials
stood behind their umpire's decision and in the record books Bill Stewart called that one right.

Actually, this is not the first time the camera has
shown an umpire's decree to be away out of line. The
St. Louis Browns almost tore up the ball park when a
foul line drive against them was ruled a home run by

the umpire of the day. Later, pictures were produced which plainly showed the ball to be somewhat removed from fair territory.

Not only did the determined Browns produce pictures of that foul ball hitting the seats but they produced affidavits to the effect. All their toil was in vain, however, as American League officials declared the judgment of the umpire to be final at the time and no decision in such an instance can be reversed. This does not apply, naturally, to a case where an arbiter gives a wrong interpretation of the rules. In happenings of this kind, the game can be re-played from the point at which the mental error occurred.

Umpires are often faced with impossible situations. During a 1949 game between the Athletics and White Sox at Comiskey Park, Gus Zernial stepped to bat with Luke Appling on first base and dropped a fly ball just inside the foul line into the right-field corner. Taft Wright gave chase but when he reached the Philadelphia bullpen he could not locate the ball. Meanwhile Zernial and Appling circled the bases.

The umpires were stumped but decided some small boy had reached out from the stands to grab the ball, so Zernial was waved back to second and Appling to third on a ground-rule double and neither man scored from that point as the A's ultimately nosed the Sox 3-2. In time the mystery was solved as relief pitcher Joe Coleman, sitting in the Athletic bullpen, admitted he had stuck the ball in his back pocket but the final result remained in the books.

A good many years ago Roger Bresnahan, famed major league catcher, was warming up a pitcher in the bullpen when he heard a ball bounce off the stands and roll toward him. Turning, he retrieved the ball and thinking it was foul he flipped it back to the infield. Umpires scratched their heads in amazement, then ruled interference on Bresnahan and called the hit a home-run. Bresnahan had a hard time living that one down.

To be a successful umpire, it appears a man must be a fine physical specimen. That pro football players, bruisers of the first degree, make able umps is proved by two men in blue operating at the same time in the American League. They are Cal Hubbard and Hank Soar, two of the greatest professionals to play cash-and-carry football in the National Football League. There is just no pushing around of Cal and Hank as both are proven rocks of Gibraltar from the rugged grid game.

Bill Summers was another of the rough-tough clan of umpires who graduated to baseball from the boxing ring. As a lightweight, Bill enjoyed a degree of success around Pawtucket, Rhode Island, and for relaxation he would watch local kids play sandlot baseball. One afternoon, he was called upon to umpire a game—a request everybody ducked for a cracked skull was usually payment for the job.

Because of his reputation as a fighter, Bill was urged to accept the assignment. He did and actually kept peace on the dangerous diamond for a couple of hours. At the end he collected three dollars in pay for a job well done.

The three bucks started Bill Summers on a career of umpiring that lasted more than 30 years. "I figured it was easier risking an attack here and there on the diamond than it was ducking ten blows a minute in the squared circle," chuckled Umpire Summers.

You must admit that the umpire earns his pay which averaged from $8,000 to $10,000 yearly at last glance. Never must the suspicion of bribery be even hinted at when mentioning umpires. John McGraw of the Giants sought to start off relations with young Bill Klem on friendly terms, away back when, so Mr. Muggsy presented Klem with a fancy balls-and-strikes indicator.

Klem rewarded McGraw with a kindly thank you and then took his position behind the plate. Later in the game McGraw protested rather strenuously against a Klem decision. The honest umpire would have none of that; quickly he tossed McGraw out of the game. P.S. Bill Klem kept the gift.

Venerable Beans Reardon of the National League has had his share of scrapes umpiring in the big show, and also in the little show. One time in the minors Reardon was chased clear out of the ball park by a knife-waving fan. Beans wasn't safe until a group of ball players pounced on the hell-bent-for-murder rooter and subdued him.

Summing up his career, Beans Reardon notes that he has ducked rocks, pop bottles, rubbish and even straw hats. He confesses, "When I became an umpire my mother cried."

Nobody ever handled an umpire with such contempt as did Bill Dahlen, star pitcher with the early Brooklyn Dodgers. On this afternoon, Dahlen really gave a roasting to Hank O'Day, one of the most famous men in blue of that time. Dahlen did everything within the boundaries of decency to incite O'Day's ire, all to no avail.

Finally, in desperation, Bill stamped right on the foot of the umpire. O'Day did not bat an eyelash. Then Dahlen threw dirt directly into the face of honest Hank. Still O'Day kept his silence. There was a reason for this peculiar behavior.

Before the game, Bill Dahlen had asked Hank O'Day how far a man could go with an umpire before he would be tossed out of the game. O'Day politely told him. Then why didn't O'Day bounce Dahlen from the ball park? He was aware of Dahlen's motives, knowing the pitcher was dying to be chased so he could continue on straight to the racetrack. "You'll stay and play baseball this hot afternoon if it kills me," declared O'Day.

Years later Frankie Frisch tried a similar ruse in the same ball park, Ebbets Field. Although Frankie was managing Pittsburgh he lived in the suburbs of New York where he spent a good deal of time cultivating his flowers, a fact pretty well known around the league. Also well remembered around the league was the fact that Frankie was bounced from as many ball games as any of his equally fiery contemporaries.

Frisch's team had engaged in a twin-bill with the Brooklyns this afternoon and early in the first game Frankie dashed on the field to deliver a blistering protest to Umpire George Barr over a comparatively minor decision.

Frankie fully expected to be banished on the spot so he stopped talking to let Umpire George Barr do the job. Frankie was impatient to get going. "Oh no you don't, Frankie," scolded Barr who had been warned against such action by Frisch. "You stick around the ball field here. Plant those posies in your garden some other day."

The name Frankie Frisch and umpires seem to go together like ham and actors. Let somebody tell a funny umpire story and chances are fearless Frankie will be involved. Although even the men in blue respected Frankie's clowning, they nevertheless dealt with him severely on occasion.

Not so was the case, though, during the 1945 season when Frankie Frisch, manager of the Pirates, was chased from the ball game two days in a row.

On the third day the Pirates showed up at the Polo Grounds with the same set of umpires in charge. No sooner had the first pitch of the game been delivered, than Frankie chose to smash a bat against the side of the Pittsburgh bat rack, creating a most annoying disturbance. Plate umpire Lou Jorda ignored the incident.

Came the second pitch and again Frankie Frisch went through the crash-bang performance. Although Jorda gave an annoying glance, he said nothing. The same thing happened on the third pitch and this was too much for umpire Jorda. He whipped off his mask and whirled on frolicking Frankie but before the man in blue could utter a sound, Frisch offered an alibi. Shouting to the reporters in the press box, Mr. Frisch declared "I just wanted to wake you fellows up."

Umpire Lou Jorda could do nothing but laugh at Manager Frisch so Frankie missed the distinction of having himself kicked out of a ball game for three days running.

When Red Ormsby was umpiring in the American League he had a favorite yarn he enjoyed relating about a companion man in blue. This umpire was having an exceedingly tough time with balls and strikes and the hometown fans were hopping on him verbally and hooting him like a houseful of owls.

Suddenly, from behind home plate came the loud, screeching voice of a female whose high-pitched voice cut to the far corners of the ball park. "If you were my husband I'd give you poison," she screamed.

Slowly the umpire turned around. He doffed his cap in gentlemanly fashion and retorted, "Madame, if you were my wife, I'd take it."

Art Passarella was a young enough umpire to be inducted into the Army during World War II. Naturally, the former American League strike-and-ball caller drew the assignment of tutoring a special detail of G.I.'s for umpiring assignments in service games.

Telling the rookie arbiters to be forceful, Passarella advised against taking back-talk from anybody on the field. "Keep the games moving along swiftly and make your decisions decisive," added Art.

"Supposing a man acts up," suggested a soldier student. "We can't kick him out of the army."

Passarella admitted that was true, but added, "We can put him on K.P., can't we?"

Nobody rode umpires rougher than did the fans baseball knew before the turn of the century. In 1899 Hank O'Day called a game at St. Louis. Although Hank was as honest and efficient as umpires come, the local rooters resented his judgment. They actually chased him off the field and into the clubhouse.

Although Hank was visibly shaken, he turned and bravely stood off the fanatical fans, at least until one guy stepped forward with a rope. This was too much even for a fearless fellow like Hank O'Day. Fortunately, as Hank counted his remaining minutes on this earth, police raced to the rescue and with drawn revolvers probably saved the life of the harrassed arbiter.

This is one occasion at least on which the fans meant it when they cried, "Kill the umpire!"

Life Begins At 40

It's a tragic thing about baseball, about all sports for that matter. The better a man learns his trade, the more inept he becomes. That is to say he knows how to make the moves better but he can't take those moves because his legs lose their spring, his eyes don't focus like they did when he was a spry youngster, and his arm creaks at the hinge. In the business world a man generally becomes a junior executive at 35 or thereabouts; in the baseball world a man usually starts slipping down the ladder of success at 35.

An exception to the rule could be pitchers and it's a sad thing in a way. By the time a scatter-armed fire-balling guy begins to control his money arm the wing drops in dollar value for the old zip is gone by then. Think of how many hurlers spend ten or more years in the minor loops learning to pitch and finally graduate into the big leagues at 30 or over. Sure they make good, but much of their potential career is gone, behind them, beyond capture.

Jim Konstanty flopped in the majors, bounced around in the minors, and returned to the National League in his thirties to practically pitch the Phillies to a pennant in 1950 as one of the all-time great relief artists. In fact, he made more mound appearances than any other hurler in the league's history. Sal Maglie, Giant hurler, reached stardom at 34, his progress handicapped severely by a Mexican League exile. Whitlow Wyatt became an all-time Dodger ace pitcher at 30 plus after finally finding himself in the minors.

Perhaps the champ longevity performer of all was little Rabbit Maranville. You'd think it would take a guy with a backlog of brawn to serve 27 years in the national pastime, but Rabbit was more drawn than brawn, never tapping the scales at anything better than 150. For the records, Rabbit Maranville got his start with the Braves of 1912 and he was serving in the minors as late as 1939. Actually Rabbit served time in the minors before 1912 so you can see he wore the active baseball suit a long, long time. He does hold the major mark for length of service with 24 seasons. At 44 he still was playing second-base for the Braves in 1935.

At the start of the 1950 season, the Detroit Tigers tried desperately to make a deal for their veteran right-hander, Paul Dizzy Trout. Trout was considered through, washed up. Only because the Tigers were short on experienced moundsmen, they kept Dizzy on the staff, otherwise he certainly would have been handed his walking papers. Not having too deep a pitching sack in which to reach, manager Red Rolfe pulled out the name of Dizzy Trout one day and started him in a crucial game.

Dizzy won a hurling pitching duel on that fine afternoon and he was on his way, almost to spark the Tigers to a pennant nobody figured they could win. Had Red Rolfe another Dizzy Trout he might have done it with a team green as grass in spots and weak on reserves. Oh, yes, Dizzy turned in his brilliant 1950 pitching, among his best, at the no longer tender age of 36. Bobo Newsom was another guy almost as ageless. Bobo for a long time chucked a baseball for different teams around the country, for more than anything else—except perhaps talking—Old Bobo loved to play ball. That Bobo was as good at 39 as at 29, Bucky Harris, Yankee manager of 1947 strongly maintained for in that season, 39-year-old Newsom did help pitch the New Yorkers to a pennant. Jimmy Dykes is another guy who stuck around baseball for a long time remaining active until he was 44. The White Sox seem to grow them tough—look at the way Luke Appling carried on year in and year out.

Grover Cleveland Alexander was of course a well mellowed 39 when he whiffed the mighty Tony Lazzeri with the bases bulging to win the 1926 World Series for the Cards over the Yanks. As a matter of fact, quite a few of the all-time greats seemed even to improve with age. When the fastball slows up, the pitching brain of necessity takes on added speed. Witness the work of not-so-rapid Robert Feller in his last few big league years.

With Pete Alexander it was always greatness; in his 41st year, Alex won 16 games and dropped nine for the 1928 Cardinals. The season of 1934 saw Alexander again on the Cardinal hurling corps and at the very twilight of his career, Old Pete was good enough to win four games at the unbelievable age of 47.

Back in the Giant days of Bill Terry, the New Yorkers had a pretty good pitching prospect in bespectacled Jack Salveson. The right-hander looked like a sure thing to gain a permanent place with the boys from Coogan's Bluff, but he faded in time from the picture.

By 1950 Jack Salveson hadn't crashed a big-league

box score in years. In major-league cities he was forgotten but not out in the Pacific Coast League. There in his 18th season of organized baseball, Jack Salveson was a ball of fire. By mid-season, Salveson had chalked up eleven wins against one setback and at the age of 36 definitely rated another major-league trial, especially with the armed service drain on the nation's youth.

Every Yankee fan of yesteryear cherishes with a warm spot the memory of Wilcy Moore. As far as relief pitchers go, Wilcy ranked right up there with the best—perhaps he was the most noble bull-penner of them all and that includes stickouts such as Joe Page, Jim Konstanty, Joe Black and Luis Arroyo, to name the more modern, when relieving really became a high-paying art.

Wilcy came directly to the Yanks from deep in the bushes at Greenville of the Sally League where he hung up the impressive mark of 30 wins and 4 losses in a single season. Not much was known about Wilcy before he joined the Yanks except that he had plenty of nothing and he looked a lot older than the thirty he claimed. "This is a pitcher?" the Yanks asked almost to a man as Moore lobbed his fast one in after donning a Ruth suit.

But old Wilcy showed them that season, 1927, by hanging up 19 wins, although he showed them little in the season after that. However in 1927 Wilcy Moore was hot. In the first game of the World Series in which the Yanks swept four in a row from the Pirates, reliever Wilcy Moore stepped right out and saved a game for Waite Hoyt, a game won by the Yankees 5-4.

Cy Moore tossed his sinker ball in 50 games for the Yankees that season and great things were predicted for the bald-headed veteran. Wilcy Moore, though, let his advocates down by flashing nothing thereafter.

When Yankee manager Miller Huggins started Wilcy Moore in the fourth game of the 1927 World Series he created the sort of surprise, though to a lesser degree, as that created by Philadelphia Philly manager Eddie Sawyer when he tossed reliever Jim Konstanty against the Yanks in the first game of the 1950 Fall Classic.

Like Konstanty, Moore twirled a good game but he won his, beating the Pirates 4-3 to wrap up the Series although Wilcy was more generous with hits, allowing ten. But Pirate pitcher John Miljus was even more generous, sending in the winning run in the ninth on a wild pitch, insuring Wilcy Moore of his Series conquest.

Another ancient ace carried his effectiveness into old age via baseball's fountain of youth. He was Walter Johnson, known equally well as the Big Train. During 19 of his 21 seasons in the major leagues, Johnson toiled for hapless Washington. Then at 37 came the Big Train's big moment. Capping a career that saw him chalk up 413 wins and 3,497 strikeouts, Walter Johnson during that memorable season pitched the Nats to a pennant. The 37-year-old Johnson won 23 games in 1924 for youthful manager Bucky Harris, the boy wonder.

Unfortunately for the Big Train, he lost his first two Series starts to the Giants by scores of 4-3 in 12 innings of the first game and 6-2 in the fifth contest. The New

Yorkers who seemed to have their hitting hats on against Johnson couldn't accomplish too much damage in this 1924 World Series against the rest of the Washington, so at the end of six games the teams stood three-all.

The Giants of 1924 had such a balanced team with such stalwarts in the infield as Bill Terry, Frank Frisch, Travis Jackson, and Heinie Groh or Freddie Lindstrom at third. George Kelly, Bill Southworth, Hack Wilson and Ross Youngs made up a formidable outfield with Hank Gowdy behind the plate. Joe Judge, Bucky Harris, Roger Peckinpaugh and Ossie Bluege is the way Washington lined up across the inner defense while Goose Goslin, Earl McNeely and Sam Rice patrolled the pastures. Muddy Ruel wore mask and mitt.

That old Walter Johnson would fail to win his long-sought World Series victory in 1924 competition seemed apparent to a sentimentally saddened nation as the Giants went ahead in the seventh game 3-1 against lefthander George Mogridge and reliever Fred Marberry. It did not seem Johnson would even get a chance to pitch, as the cause looked lost.

The Senators had one last, dying gasp left and they made it count by pushing across a pair of counters on a fluke bounder as they knotted the score at 3-all in the bottom of the eighth. At this juncture, Boy Wonder Bucky Harris waved a hand to the bullpen and beckoned the great one, Walter Johnson.

"Stop them in the ninth," begged Bucky, "and we'll win it."

The Big Train tried hard. He nailed frisky Freddie

Lindstrom but fighting Frankie Frisch whistled a triple and it looked as though Johnson were headed for a third World Series loss.

Somehow, though, the old guys have a way of winning the big ones. Johnson gave up a walk to Ross Youngs and then bore down on George Kelly. A mighty roar bounced across the field as the big train raced past Kelly to strike out the Giant stickman. It seemed like child's play then for Johnson to retire Meusel on an infield tap to close out the round.

Through the ninth and tenth of the seventh and sudden-death World Series game rolled the Giants and Senators, neither able to sever the three-run deadlock. In the eleventh, Walter Johnson had to reach for every resource he possessed. Two Giants were on base, nobody was out and the picture loomed black, very black. Any old timer will tell you that Walter Johnson proceeded to paint one of the masterpieces of Series play by striking out Lindstrom, Frisch and Kelly.

The last of the 12th of the 1924 Fall Classic is something Giant fans like to skip over in speaking of the past. With one out, Muddy Ruel popped into foul territory and like a tiger Hank Gowdy lunged for the ball. He located it and lost it the last second when he stepped into his own mask and stumbled. Given another opportunity to hit, Muddy produced a dangerous double. With the cheers of the throng filling his ears, Walter Johnson slapped a gentle grounder Travis Jackson way and unbelievably slick-fielding Travis booted the ball putting runners on first and third with still one out.

Giant pitcher Bentley probably decided he was fate's unluckiest child when, after getting outfielder McNeely to drill a perfect double-play ball down to Freddie Lindstrom at third, he saw the sphere take a crazy hop and skip easily beyond Lindstrom's reach while Muddy Ruel waltzed in from third with the winning run of a 4-3 victory. In a way both McNeely and Walter Johnson deserved the break for it was McNeely's horrendous boot that brought defeat to Johnson in the first Series tilt.

And the hero of the Series? Well, although he won only one game and that in relief, Walter Johnson grabbed the laurels. A well-earned honor, to be sure, for an old man of 37 considered over the hill on the pitching mound!

The saga of Walter Johnson, the older man, does not end at this point. If the Big Train sparkled plenty in the last game of the 1924 World Series, he beamed even brighter during the entire 1925 classic when Washington met Pittsburgh, at least until the seventh and deciding game. Now 38 years old, Johnson won his first two starts against the Pirates, permitting the Smoky City slickers only one lone run in the two tilts. Down three games to one, Pittsburgh staged one of the most remarkable comebacks in World Series memory by taking the next two to even the count at three games apiece.

Naturally it fell upon the aged but unstooped shoulders of wonderful Walter Johnson to halt the Pirate surge in the seventh game. Walt drew for an opponent Vic Aldridge, hurling with only two days of rest thereby making the big Choo Choo a big bet to join the select group of chuckers who have won three games in Series play. Aldridge, by the way, was also gunning for win number three having bested the Senators 3-2 in the second game and 6-3 in the fifth.

That there would be no third victory was disclosed in the very first inning when Washington scored four times to batter Aldridge from the box. Johnson's chances too took a dip to the depths in the third as Walter allowed the Pirates to bounce back with a trio of tallies. In the seventh Pittsburgh pulled even 6-6 thanks no little to Roger Peckinpaugh who dropped a cinch pop fly.

Making up somewhat for his grievous misplay, Peck powered a round-tripper in the top of the eighth. Rain splattered the field and observers report that Walter Johnson seemed to develop trouble in controlling the ball. At any rate, another Peckinpaugh error permitted Pittsburgh to score thrice in the last of the eighth to cop the final game of the classic 9-7.

Pity goes to poor Peckinpaugh. Usually a flawless fielder, Roger ruined whatever chance Johnson had to wrap up three Series victories at a late 38. Peckinpaugh, himself, earned the dubious distinction in 1925 of becoming the only player to commit eight errors in a World Series. And all this, mind you, occurred a few days after Roger had been selected the American League's Most Valuable Player!

Walter Johnson fares much better in the record books. The 38-year-old codger really had it in the first game when he whiffed ten Pirates and permitted only five safeties to shackle the Bucs 4-1. Then in the fourth contest he hurled his shutout, allowing the powerful Corsair crew only six safeties this time.

Talk about old men in baseball and the conversation is bound to get around to a couple of colorful codgers of the Dodgers who finished out their big-league lives not so long ago. One of the winning oldsters was fat and familiar Freddie Fitzsimmons and the other was long, lanky Curt Davis. Maybe Fitz was a stout and stylish 39 in 1940 but the hard-working righthander came darn near bringing Brooklyn its first pennant in 20 years by hanging up 16 victories and losing only two, a percentage record that has been tough for anyone to match! The next season Freddie slipped to six wins against one loss, but the win was a very valuable one late in the season over the pressing Cardinals as the Dodgers finally captured that pennant.

In the 1941 World Series, fat and forty Freddie took the mound against the Yankees in the third game at Ebbets Field in an effort to give the Dodgers an edge in the classic then deadlocked at one win apiece. Freddie did right well for himself holding the Yankees at bay for seven innings without a score until hard luck knocked him from the box. A line drive off a Yankee bat hit Fitz squarely on the knee in the seventh and he had to yield to huge Hugh Casey. Also on the unfortunate side for Fitzsimmons was the fact that Marius Russo, Yankee chucker, was also hot limiting the Dodgers to a lone tally and eventually winning the contest 2-1. The Yanks, by the way, took the Series four games to one, helped no little by the famous play in which Mickey Owen, Dodger catcher, allowed a third-out third strike to get away from him thereby giving the Yanks the chance they needed to wrap up a "lost" game and eventually the seven-game competition.

The World Series of 1941 marked the last great effort of Freddie Fitzsimmons for in 1942 Freddie at 41 lost his effectiveness and by June the Brooks cut him loose from the squad.

Curt Davis made his entrance into this world at Greenfield, Missouri, in the year 1906. After a promising pitching career with the Phils, Cards, and Cubs, Curt joined the Dodgers and showed good, reliable stuff. In 1942 Curt was a nicely rounded 36 and considered in some quarters to be ready for the right-arm boneyard. That season, 1942, was the one in which the Brooks won 104 and not the pennant as the Redbirds copped, although Curt Davis did his best to bring the bunting to Brooklyn by turning in some 15 wins while dropping only six to show a magnificent earned run average of 2.36 in 32 games. As a matter of fact, another aging ace, southpaw Larry French, finished the same Dodger season with a 15-4 figure.

As for Curt Davis, he led Dodger pitchers in 1944 with a 10-11 mark, not a notable figure but then the Dodgers of 1944 were lucky to win any games. And for an old-timer of 38, well, Curt's ten victories were well nigh terrific. The year 1946 saw Curtis B. Davis exit from big-league box scores. Now 40, poor Curt compiled his worst major mark. Appearing in only two innings of 1946 as a Dodger, Davis compiled an enormous earned run average of 13.50. However, in view of Curt's earlier achievements this figure can be kindly ignored.

It was the World Series of 1940 and Cincinnati entered the ferocious fray against Detroit's Tigers without the services of star catcher Ernie (Schnozz) Lombardi. The big moose had been laid low late in the season by a painful wound sustained under pennant-drive fire. Out of the dugout and into the catcher's tools stepped veteran receiver Jimmy Wilson, a fattish and forty hustler of yore. Jimmy astonished everybody including himself by catching every game of the seven except the third, handled by big Lom. However, had Ernie recovered his health fully it is doubtful whether he could have nudged red-hot Jimmy Wilson from backstopping duties.

At forty, Jimmy became the star of the '40 Fall Classic. His nifty hitting, .353, and his sprightly catching paced the Cincinnati Reds to a Series victory, the same Rhineland gang which had dropped four in a row to the Yanks a season earlier. To top off a magnificent World Series show, Jimmy stole the only base the Reds pilfered in the seven game setto.

Here was an old guy coming through and how, probably playing his best baseball at the age of 40 and in the physically toughest position—behind the plate. "You think he's good now," cracked one wiseacre. "Wait'll you see Jimmy in action at 50!"

At 41 Luke Appling was still making himself useful in the infield for the Chicago White Sox. More than somewhat under-rated, Luke has always been a .300 hitter and an extremely accomplished shortstop with a good arm and adequate speed afoot. Luke is one of those happy-go-lucky characters known, oddly enough, as the groaner to his teammates. Perhaps

Luke's continued success might be attributed to his attitude toward the game. He hardly ever knows how well he is batting, which means he doesn't lose sleep and efficiency like most players worrying over prolonged batting slumps. In fact, Luke never had many such hitless stages, and when he left the Sox in 1951 to manage the Memphis Chicks, he was as spry as ever.

The Brooklyn Dodgers of 1922 were not so powerful they couldn't have used a little additional pitching support. As a matter of fact, the Dodgers, as was their custom in those days, were floundering aimlessly in the second division. It must have been a deep source of pain and embarrassment to the management to see an old workhorse like Jeff Pfeffer winning 19 games and dropping only 12 for the high-flying Redbirds of St. Louis. The Brooks, you see, had cast out Pfeffer as a washed out old man, yet he bounced back to lead all hurlers on what probably added up to the league's best mound corps. How those old guys can haunt you!

In 1950 the Yanks pleaded with huge John Mize to please go back to Kansas City and make room for some guy who could play first-base regularly. "Give me the job," demanded Mize and manager Stengel was forced to acquiesce. What John Mize at a delicate 37 did for the Yanks of '50 reads like something out of Merriwell. He went into hitting spurts that surpassed anything accomplished before in his long and brilliant National League stay. And without John's home run punch it is doubtful indeed whether the Yanks would have won the flag!

Mystery of Myths

It was in the 1932 World Series and reliable Charley Root was chucking for the Chicago Cubs against the New York Yankees. The great Babe majestically took two strikes, acknowledging each pitch with a flourish. Next move in the Ruth saga was to lift his left hand in the direction of the right-centerfield stands. Root pitched and Babe swung; a mighty drive sailed far and high, precisely in the direction of those same distant stands. The Babe, they said, had called his shot.

Only, like most baseball stories this one has its other side. Gabby Hartnett, Cub catcher of the day, claims the Babe never indicated he would rap a homer into those stands. Gabby should know; he was closer to the Babe than anyone and Hartnett was never a gentleman to deny a popular figure his just due. However, even if Ruth did not call his round-tripper it still was a timely blow—one of the Babe's amazing figure of 15 circuit clouts in 10 World Series.

No doubt the Dodgers really earned their claim to the title, "daffiness boys," especially during the halcyon régime of beloved manager Wilbert Robinson. Robby's Robins did screwy things like passing each other on the basepaths and winding up a trio at third base; however, contrary to popular belief, Babe Herman was never hit on the head by a fly ball. At least big Babe says he never was.

Since 1939, with only one exception, the Dodgers have been a consistent first-division ball club. For heads-up baseball you can't find a better group of infield representatives than guys like Pee Wee Reese, Jackie Robinson, Billy Herman, Arkie Vaughan, Dolf Camilli or Gil Hodges. Yet, let the Dodgers do something just the least bit awkward and immediately comes the comment, "They're at it again—those daffy Dodgers."

Longtime baseball observers will relate how a composed crew like the Yankees of the Ruth-Gehrig invincible era committed a boner fully as fantastic as any Dodger passing another Brook on the basepaths. And the enormous oversight was committed by no less a star than Larrupin' Lou Gehrig, though truth to tell the renowned first-sacker was not entirely at fault.

The zany incident took place at Griffith Stadium, Washington, early in the 1931 season when Gehrig rammed a Fred Marberry pitch deep into the stands for a pat home run. As is the custom, Lou trotted around the basepaths behind shortstop Lynn Lary who had been roosting on first base. Lary, however, didn't concede Gehrig the homer; the Yankee baserunner thought one of Washington's outfielders had grabbed the ball for an out, so after crossing third base he headed back for his shortstop position picking up his glove en route.

With his mates trying to get his attention, Gehrig heard only the roar of the crowd. Hence, he stamped hard on home plate only to manufacture an automatic out for passing Lynn Lary on the basepaths. To be sure, Lynn Lary was the more guilty party than Gehrig, but had a Brooklyn Dodger been involved in this bit of heads-down base-running, surely his fame would have lingered for generations.

To his dying day, Fred Merkle will insist he was not the goat of the infamous Giant-Cub Polo Grounds game that ultimately cost the New Yorkers the pennant of 1908. Many baseball fans and most players of that day will agree with Fred.

"I only wish folks will forget about that game," moaned Merkle throughout the years.

A young first-baseman, Merkle subbed for ailing Fred Tenney as the Giants took the field against the first-place Cubs on the afternoon of September 23, 1908 at the Polo Grounds. The Giants needed this one game to clinch the pennant and since the game ended 2-1 on a ninth inning single by Al Bridwell it appeared to everybody as though the New Yorkers had wrapped up the flag.

The ordinary finish was in itself a genuine spine-tingler. There had been two out and Moose McCormick was on third with Merkle on first. On Bridwell's solid single, Merkle stopped short of second, watching the winning run score and sprinted along with his happy teammates for the dugout.

However, Johnny Evers, Cubs second-baseman, had been watching Merkle. As soon as he saw Fred take off, he called for the ball. Chicago left fielder Artie Hoffman snatched the ball from a fan and tossed it to Joe Tinker who relayed it to Evers. The Cub infielder stepped on second and Merkle was automatically forced thereby nullifying the winning run of the Giants.

Naturally bedlam broke loose and protests were fired back and forth across the desk of the league president. The judgment of the umpire, as always, prevailed and the game was ordered replayed. Stamping themselves as genuine opportunists, the Chicago men squashed the Giants in the playoff and won the pennant.

Merkle has never accepted the verdict. "Stopping the game as soon as the winning run was scored had always been the custom of the day," protested Fred. "I was more of a scapegoat than a goat." His manager, John McGraw, always stood by Fred maintaining steadily that Merkle was never a goat of any sorts.

Because he chased fleet-footed Eddie Collins all the way to home plate and lost the race, Giant third-baseman Heinie Zimmerman has gone down in baseball's archives as the dumb Dutchman. The gifted run permitted the White Sox to down the Giants 4-2 in the 1917 World Series clincher and stamped Heinie as a bit of a blunderer.

Truth to tell, Heinie was absolutely blameless. His mates had left home plate as unprotected as a cat at a dogshow and poor Heinie could find nobody to throw the ball to. So he set out after Collins in futile flight. The real offenders were pitcher Rube Benton or first-baseman Walter Holke, neither of whom had the good judgment to go home. Giant catcher Raredin also was not in the vicinity of home plate.

Some chroniclers of baseball have also attempted to hang goat horns on White Sox pitcher Urban Faber, although Faber was on the winning side in the same series and could not possibly have been a nanny of any sort. Urban actually did commit a fantastic faux pas which will keep intact his memory in all World Series discussions.

In the fifth inning of the second game of the 1917 Series, Urban Faber decided to steal third base which was all well and good except for one thing: Faber's teammate Weaver was occupying third base. Nevertheless, pitcher Faber went on to win three games in that World Series, the third as a relief hurler in the fifth tilt, while dropping but one contest. So Urban Faber emerged from the classic as one of the big heroes, not as a goat!

To be sure, the 1917 World Series, won by the White Sox four games to two, was wild and woolly in many respects. White Sox outfielder Johnny Collins could easily have been a goat; he muffed two fly balls in the third game. However, as in the case of Urban Faber, Johnny Collins was on the winning side.

Ernie Lombardi, outstanding National League catcher for many seasons, unwittingly provided World Series comedy relief in 1939, certainly through no fault of his own. The Yankees were pouring across the winning runs of the fourth and deciding game in Cincinnati when big Lom set himself to take an out-field throw and put the tag on Charley Keller. King Kong, no midget himself, ploughed into lumbering Lombardi and flattened the big Cincy catcher. Thus with the ball resting inches from the fingerprints of flattened Ernie Lombardi, Joe DiMaggio also romped across the plate, coming in all the way from third base!

Why didn't Lombardi get up, grasp the ball and put it on DiMag? Nobody could supply the answer and the Ernie episode was cause for much merriment. The fact of the case is Lombardi had been knocked colder than an anemic Eskimo, although he modestly never offered an alibi. His Cincinnati co-workers of the day will tell you though that 50 runners could have raced across the plate before Ernie was in any condition to pick up that ball and put the tag on the last one.

Had Louis Evans played rightfield for the Dodgers of the Robinson era he probably could have achieved a greater degree of fame than he did with the Cardinals of 1909. Here again was a daffiness of a sort to make the Brooklynites look like a bunch of brain-trusters.

In those days it was the Evans custom to play a deep—very deep right field. Texas Leaguers were dropping with some regularity right in front of him and everybody wondered how come until the day it was discovered Evans played his position to take best advantage of the shade from the grandstand. His ruse discovered, Evans next tried to play the outfield with a sun umbrella but he was overruled by the umpires of the era.

The umbrella incident of Evans brings to mind the raincoat of Connie Ryan, also never a Dodger. At the time Connie covered second for the Boston Braves of 1949. In a crucial end-of-season double-header against those Dodgers, the Braves found themselves playing in a downpour deliberate enough to wash out a swimming meet. No open dates remained for replay of the game, hence the umpires ruled that the twin-bill must go on.

Connie Ryan showed his contempt for the decision and threw the gathering into an uproar by striding to the batters' box late in the afternoon, wearing, of all things, a raincoat. Like the lightning of the storm, the umpires struck down on Connie, sending him from one shower to another. Now had Connie been on the other side of the fence, on the Dodger bench to be precise, his name would be a byword in beer parlors for years to come.

Legend lists Judge Kenesaw Mountain Landis as the man who almost single-handedly saved baseball after the Black Sox scandal. The severe Judge is revered as the brain behind baseball of yesteryear, the man who almost always made the right moves.

In truth it is not too incorrect to single out Deacon Branch Rickey as the saviour of our national pastime. Without Branch Rickey and his revolutionary Cardinal farm system it is doubtful whether any minor-league clubs could have survived the darkest days of the depression.

Most major-league teams lose money on their lower farm clubs but they operate the bush branches to develop talent which pays off in the big show. To be sure, without the help of parent organizations, many a lower-league team would have folded long since. The opportunity for breaking into baseball erased, some of the game's stars would no doubt have entered other employment and their loss would have been the game's loss.

Never a Rickey supporter, Landis always sought loopholes in brother Branch's chain-gang setup and when he found one in 1938, the Judge clamped down a firm foot freeing 80 choice Cardinal farmhands including the soon-to-become-great Pete Reiser. To his dying day, Judge Landis bitterly fought Branch Rickey's farm-team project although many learned students of the game have condemned the Judge's actions as being contrary to the best interests of the organized sport.

Whatever the feeling for Rickey's revolutionary farm system, it can be said the operation did give every poor club in the league a chance to compete against richer rivals and buying star players with a fat bankroll was no longer the first factor in preparing to push for a pennant.

Time was when the McGraws and the Jake Rupperts kept domination of the national pastime in New York City. Gradually conditions changed. For proof, look at Tom Yawkey's Red Sox of the 1930's and also the 1940's when the Beantown bankroll did its utmost to purchase a pennant by paying heavy cabbage for every talented player on the market. At length, the Sox discarded the policy and won the flag only after the management began building its farm and developing its own players.

To Branch Rickey can go full credit for putting the small city on the baseball map. The close races in both leagues after World War II are a tribute to Branch's ideas about baseball farms. And those tight fights for the flag brought baseball the greatest revenues at the gate in the history of the game, another feather in the cap of Branch Rickey, not Kenesaw Mountain Landis.

Every time a fusillade of home runs breaks out in a modern ball game, the cry of "rabbit ball—deaden the horsehide" goes up from fans and sports writers alike. Still, the game seems to have been built on a lively ball (making for a lively game), for back in 1880 the balls were so juiced up in the National League it was not so uncommon for teams to score 100 runs in a single game!

On the other hand, scores have been mounting to astronomical figures in professional football and nobody has accused pigskin manufacturers of pumping helium into the oval.

Popular belief attributes to the Brooklyn Dodgers (them again) one of the most colossal collapses of a league-leader in modern history. It was the season of 1942 and the Dodgers had been picked by many sports scribes to repeat their 1941 bunting grabbing with the greatest of ease. The advance dope looked sound when the Dodgers were leading the pack by 10 full games on August 6.

However, no less an authority than Brooklyn president Larry MacPhail seemed to sense the handwriting on the wall when he predicted, "This club is not going to win the pennant." To MacPhail's crafty eye it appeared the Dodgers were not bearing down as hard as they should.

At that, who can accuse the Bums of melting under pressure, for in 1942 they won a staggering 104 games to become only the third club in modern major-league history to win 100 or more games and no pennant. The Cardinals of 1942, it is recorded, captured 43 of their last 52 games to nose the Flatbush Flock.

In spite of the terrific .813 pace they set, the Cardinals just did manage to shade the Brooks for the flag by two games. The Dodgers, far from folding, came smashing back to take their last ten games in a row, almost enough to nip the high-flying Red Birds. Any team that can bounce back into contention after frittering away a late-season ten-game can hardly be accused of getting a lump in the throat.

No less an authority than noted sports writer Jimmy Powers thinks today's baseball teams are somewhat superior to those of yesteryear. Using John McGraw as his source, Jimmy points out that most old-time teams had one or two stars "and the rest were tobacco-chewing, beer-guzzling bums." He adds that the baseball team of this age is much closer to top physical condition from bat boy to star than were the squads of "rowdies" who perpetuated the national pastime back in the early 1900's.

The Powers opinion is of course contrary to the propaganda dished out by many an old-timer who refuses to put the stars of today in the same class with the shining lights of the gaslight era. Mention Ralph Kiner and he'll tell you Home-Run Baker had no lively ball to help him reach the 50-per-season circuit-clout mark. In case memory needs refreshing, Frank Baker covered third in what at the time was known as the $100,000 infield of the Philadelphia Athletics. The club's cleanup man, Home-Run Baker led the American League in round-trippers from 1911 to 1914, with nine, ten, twelve and eight, in that order.

Granted that today's baseball may contain a bit more rabbit, the great hitters of the gay nineties or thereabouts had certain advantages on their side, too. For example, your yesteryear baseball booster may point out that of 40 players in the history of baseball to hit .400 or better, 26 turned the difficult trick before the turn of the century.

Examine the statistics more closely, however, and you'll find a number of holes in the argument of the old-timer. Prior to 1900, establishing a mark of .400 was not nearly so difficult as it is today.

Before 1880, a batter could get himself credit for a base hit if one of the base runners ahead of him deliberately ran into a batted ball. About the same period, it took a batter nine balls to gain first base. The year 1887 was really a bonanza for batters. During this season a batter was permitted four strikes before he was declared out and if he walked it counted as a base hit. No wonder so many high hitters!

The first big hitter in baseball's real initial organization was Ross Barnes who knocked the apple for .403 away back in 1876 while Adrian C. "Cap" Anson of the old Chicago White Stockings waited until 1879 to post his .407. Under baseball's laws of 1884 which favored the hitter so strongly, no less than three players topped the .400 mark. They were Fred Dunlap with .420, T. J. Esterbrook with .408 and Harry Stovey with .404.

Then came that year 1887 when the five balls and four strikes rules were in vogue with a walk counting for a hit. During that season, nine members of the American Association and three of the National League, or a total of 12 in all, batted better than .400, with one J. E. O'Neill leading the pack with an incredible .492—or almost a hit every other time at bat! Is it any wonder the old-timers looked so good in comparison to today's standouts?

Leader of the 26 who compiled averages of .400 or better up until 1900 was Jesse Burkett, called "The Crab" by his teammates. Covering the outfield for Cleveland and St. Louis, The Crab three times batted better than .400! Burkett turned the trick with Cleveland twice, posting percentages of .423 and .410 and with St. Louis once, drilling the horsehide for a fat .402. Anson, Delahanty and Thompson each hit .400 or more during two separate seasons in the National League while Stovey clicked twice on the American Association. Such scintillating stickwork today would surely attract attention in the cartoon panel of Bob Ripley's "Believe It or Not."

In modern baseball, however, with greater odds against the batter there have been few standout sluggers who have reached the .400 mark. Best of the bunch of course were Ty Cobb and Rogers Hornsby. Greatest woodman in the history of the National League, Rogers three times topped .400, in 1922 with .401, in 1924 with .424 and in 1925 with .403. The overall major-league average of Rogers the wrecker was .358.

As brilliant as Hornsby was in National League play, Ty Cobb sparkled as splendidly in his league, the American. A member of the Detroit Tigers in 1911, Cobb cracked out a .420 average. Exactly one season later he almost duplicated the feat with a .410. Somehow the Georgia Peach allowed ten long years to slip by before he notched his next 5 for 2 average, a nifty .403 in 1925. For his total big-league play, Ty Cobb showed a .367 percentage.

Among the two-time .400 toppers were George Sisler of the St. Louis Browns who punched a remarkable .407 in 1920 and an even better .420 in 1922. Probably baseball's most unlucky batsman was Shoeless Joe Jackson, of Black Sox fame, who chose 1911 to hit .408 for Cleveland, the same season Cobb was carving out his .420.

Even the hitters of modern baseball had an important factor in their favor which weighed heavily as late as 1930, the season Bill Terry of the Giants knocked out a .401 average to become the last National Leaguer to go higher than a .400. In those days the outfield fly which moved a runner up a base counted as a sacrifice and not as a time at bat. This ruling, back in effect, does boost certain averages and in reflection, makes Ted Williams' .406 of 1942 a really formidable batting achievement.

All in all, it would seem that today's diamond athletes, as a group, are better than their forerunners. Fielding records and double-play records too, continue to fall and even the modern New York Giants fractured a long-standing total home-run mark. The work of Ty Cobb on the basepaths and devastation of Babe Ruth in the batter's box shine most brightly out of the past, with Roger Maris and Maury Wills finally breaking their greatest single season records.

Every once in a while a story sweeps the sports nation about how one major-league team is stealing signals from the competition by stationing a spy in the center-field bleachers and by equipping this intruder with a powerful pair of binoculars. Advance this theory to any sound baseball man and he'll reply "Fiddlesticks."

In spite of the fact that the story is strictly old hat, shortly after Jack Onslow took over management of the White Sox he accused the Cleveland Indians of winning the 1948 pennant by such ungentlemanly methods. Nevertheless, Onslow had support for his daring declaration. During the same season, Joe Kuhel had Rick Ferrell scouring the bleachers for Indian spies because Joe was convinced some center-field spy was stealing signals from his Washington team. Kuhel never found the spy.

When Connie Mack's torrid teams were devastating rival American League pitching the spy stories made the rounds of baseball. Nobody, not even Mack's A's could hit with such authority unless he knew what was coming, argued the wise ones. Then, as later, the spy in the bleachers was never located.

Not so easily convinced was Roger Peckinpaugh, manager of the Cleveland Indians at that time. So certain was Roger that spies peered through powerful lenses to pick off signals from his catcher to his pitcher that he assigned not one man, but a detail of secret agents to flush out the Philadelphia spy. At length, Peck grudgingly admitted that the Athletics hired no spy—just good hitters.

Most big-league spying is done by the coaches and by the batters themselves. They usually seek a flaw in a pitcher's delivery, a tip-off in motion, so they know what to expect, fast ball, curve, change up. And when such a flaw is discovered, look out! Knowing what is coming up to the plate, good hitters will knock the ball to the far corners of the park!

A Laughing Matter

All of baseball's humor is not wrapped up in the loud-mouthed insults hurled at umpires from the bleachers and grandstands. Baseball has always had its own brand of humor and has probably produced some of the most comical characters extant. Oddly enough, it is usually the members or managers of a sagging second-division team who get off the heartiest quips though no reason can be advanced for such light-heartedness in the face of diamond disaster.

Of all the witty ones, Wilbur Robinson's crack about his second-division Dodger team stands out as a classic untouchable. Sadly watching the Brooks loaf through and blow another game, Uncle Robbie, manager of the Brooklynites, drolled, "Overconfidence may yet cost the Dodgers sixth place!"

Lefty Gomez of course has always been one of the most quoted wise-crackers in baseball. The story goes about how Lefty and Jimmy Dykes were having a dandy discussion about how to pitch to a batter with men on base. Lefty and Jimmy could come to no agreement and finally agreed to let Mike Kelley settle the argument. Kelley is one of the senior sages of the game.

Finding Kelley in his hotel room, Lefty pounded on the door and shouted for Mike to get up. "We have a question to ask you," begged Goofy Gomez.

"Go away, get lost." Kelley yawned through the door. "Can't you ask me some other time?"

Lefty feigned shock. "What, and leave two men on base?"

All of baseball's humor is not necessarily limited to the wisecrack. Away back in 1906, Luthor Taylor objected strongly to playing in the rain when the umpires insisted the game must go on. So Taylor took his position in the Giant coaching box nicely dressed in boots, raincoat and some sort of fisherman's hat. For his mockery, Luthor Taylor gathered a not-so-funny $25 fine from National League president Harry Pulliam.

As headman of the Cleveland Indians, hustling Bill Veeck became an idea-a-day fellow. Many of his innovations were commendable, others were chuckle-provoking. His fireworks plus perfume and orchids for the ladies brought many a grin to the faces of fans. One of Bill's biggest brainstorms was the laundry service for visiting housewives.

Bill figured out that many a housefrau would attend a ball game if she could drop off the bundle of wash before the game and pick it up later completely laundered. And Veeck went right out and set up such a service for the lady fan!

Maybe Tony Cuccinello wasn't traded from Brooklyn to Boston because of his reputation as the champ cigar smoker in all baseball. But the story is a good one and who knows, Casey Stengel is a manager often guided by impulses.

Anyhow, Tony was holding down second base for the Dodgers at the time and with Brooklyn at bat

Tony tried to advance from first to third only to be tagged out—and he was standing up yet! Coaching at third base, manager Casey Stengel almost swallowed his choppers. "Why didn't you slide?" he raved at Cooch.

Tony appeared shocked. "What," he said with some surprise, "and break my cigars." The very next season saw Tony Cuccinello playing second base for the Boston Braves.

Casey Stengel is one of those whip wits who will always be remembered for humor in baseball. Perhaps the most famous tale concerning Case involves Hack Wilson, the chunky outfielder covering the Ebbets Field outer grass also at a time when Casey was managing the futile flock.

On this particular afternoon, Walter (Boom Boom) Beck was being Boom-boomed on the Flatbush mound to such an extent even patient Stengel could no longer witness the carnage. Stengel tried to get Boom Boom out of the box, but Beck insisted he was all right and had plenty of stuff. In desperation, the Dodger pilot tried to get the ball away from his floundering pitcher.

Boom Boom Beck exploded and got off his best pitch of the afternoon, a high hard one that bounced off the rightfield wall more than 250 feet away. Hack Wilson was quietly sunning himself in the Ebbets Field sun when he saw the ball bounce back past him. Hustling all the way, Hack pounced on the ball and pegged a perfect strike into second base. Everybody remained dumbfounded until Casey Stengel came to life with a zip and ordered Hack Wilson to join Boom

Boom Beck in the showers. Poor Hack was just doing his best to remain a little longer around the major leagues.

If you are a youthful baseball fan you might think it has been dozens of decades since baseball players last supported sizeable mustaches and yes, even beards. You might think so, but you would be wrong. (The House of David is excluded from this paragraph of course.)

It all happened in Brooklyn (What again?) back in 1936. Frenchy Bordagary showed up wearing not only a fuzzy mustache but a gaudy goatee as well. And that's how Frenchy played the outfield, there being no regulation against such facial attire. The story goes that Frenchy grew the mustache originally for a picture part he had been playing out in Hollywood during the off-season.

There may be a reason why ballplayers of today don't wear whiskers. With so many bonus babies having joined the majors at one point, half the players probably haven't yet begun to shave.

No place in the ballpark appears to be 100 per cent safe, least of all the bench. Ask hurler Jack Bruner who was knocked out while sitting on the Chicago White Sox bench.

Bruner and Randy Gumpert, another moundsman, were squatting on the bullpen bench when Gumpert hopped up to watch an exciting play at Yankee Stadium. The bench tilted and Jack landed smack on the ground, hard enough to injure his elbow and to prevent him from doing any pitching at all for quite a few days!

In his well-known comedy act, Al Schact, the clown prince of baseball, pulls a hot-dog sequence that is actually based on fact, though few people know this. The scene takes place in a bullpen where relief pitcher Schact presumably is called on to warm up. He goes through the motions while taking an occasional bite out of the dog. Suddenly he gets the signal to enter the game.

"Who's coming up?" Al asks.

"Gehrig, Ruth and Dickey," replies his catcher solemnly.

"Don't let anybody touch my hot dog," declares the clown prince. "I'll be right back."

Actually the barb is said to have been pulled first by a Yankee—relief pitcher Henry Johnson. As in the routine of Al Schact, Johnson was warming up in the bullpen while munching on a hot dog when he got the summons to the mound. Like Schact, Henry asked, "Who's coming up?"

He was told, "Mickey Cochrane, Al Simmons and Jimmy Foxx."

"Keep an eye on my hot dog," Johnson quick-quipped. "I'll be right back." You can guess the outcome. Henry Johnson did come right back to finish his hot dog.

The story is told about shortstop Dick Culler who performed with a variety of National League clubs including the Braves, Cubs and Giants. A flash with the Braves of 1945, Dick was having one of those off-years, so common to many good players, in 1947. As a result, Sibby Sisti took over Dick's shortstopping chores. In one game the Braves were getting their ears pinned back so Boston manager Bill Southworth decided to give Culler a workout at short.

"What's the score?" asked manager Southworth.

"We're losing by 9-2," somebody piped up.

"Sit down, Dick," Southworth snapped at Culler. "We ain't giving up yet!"

Yogi Berra of the Yanks is a sort of baseball Sam Goldwyn. Yogi, you see, not only murders opposing pitchers but he murders the King's English as well. On one occasion, somebody asked Yogi the Yank about his batting average. "Last time I took a look," replied the Yog, "it was exactly .290 unless they took something off for social security."

Nobody was more surprised to see a red hen playing centerfield in Comiskey Park, Chicago, than Detroit centerfielder Roger (Doc) Cramer. After all, centerfield was supposed to have been Doc's post.

At any rate, Kramer gave chase to the intruder and while fans howled he captured the frightened fowl and handed the cackling gal over to a park attendant. After the game Doc inspected the hen and found a tag attached to the clucker reading, "This is intended as a gift for the winner." Without hesitation, Roger handed the hen over to pitcher Earl Caldwell who had blanked the Pale Hose 5-0 that afternoon!

No screwier character ever made an appearance on the baseball scene than Charles Lupica, rabid rooter for the Cleveland Indians. Late in May when his Indians were in seventh place, fearless Charles made a wager he would sit atop a four-foot platform on a 20-foot pole hoisted above his drugstore, until the Indians won the pennant. And he did.

From May 31 until September 25 — exactly 117 days—Lupica straddled that flagpole, breaking in fact the record of 71 days for flag-pole sitting set by Shipwreck Van Nolan. In appreciation, Indian owner Bill Veeck conducted ceremonies for his number-one-fanatic at Municipal Stadium, presenting Lupica with a new car. What convinced Charles his campaign was in vain and that all was lost for the Cleveland Club was a mock funeral with a horse-drawn hearse at which the Indian players buried the flag they had captured the season before.

Talented third-baseman Bobby Brown tells this story of Yogi Berra. Boning up for his medical examinations, Doc Brown carried along on a road trip a volume on "The Human Anatomy." (How Yogi who reads only comic books at best and Bobby who is one of baseball's most studious men ever became roommates poses quite a mystery.)

Anyhow, Yogi watched Bobby pouring through his book on anatomy and when Bobby finally laid it aside Yogi eagerly asked, "Tell me, Bobby, how did the story turn out?"

Everybody knows what happened when Col. Jake Ruppert tried to slice the salary of his star southpaw Lefty Gomez after a particularly disastrous season by El Goofo. Enraged at watching Lefty win only 11 games while dropping 15 the previous season Ruppert threatened to cut Gomez from $25,000 to a pitiful $7,500.

Lefty of course was shocked. "Listen Colonel," Gomez blandly suggested. "Tell you what. You keep the salary and give me the cut."

Before Eric McNair died of a heart attack he and Doc Cramer were great buddies, fellows who would go to great ends for a laugh. To win friendly wagers McNair would dive into Lake Michigan with all his clothes on and once he let them shave all the hair off his head in the middle of a baseball season.

Once after a combination luncheon-cocktail party, Eric and Doc showed up at the ballpark late and slightly tipsy but neither let on and Cramer took over his usual center-field post. Notwithstanding his glow, Doc Cramer pounded out four consecutive hits. McNair could not believe his slightly glassy eyes, so at length he turned on his pal and growled, "Doc, when in blazes are you going to sober up?"

Enter again Casey Stengel, the younger Case but not the less funny Case. It was the World Series of 1922 and because of an injured heel he had been wearing a sponge in the back of his shoe. Racing for the plate, Casey felt sure he was losing his shoe for the lace had become untied but he gave it an all-out slide to safety anyhow.

Still stretched in the dust, Casey looked up to the next hitter, Hank Gowdy, and remarked, "Boy was I lucky to score. I just lost my shoe going around third base."

Hank looked at Stengel's feet and saw two shoes, one on each foot. "How many shoes did you start with?" Hank asked.

Every once in a while a shaggy dog story makes the baseball rounds. One of the more recent concerns a talking hound who stopped in a neighborhood pub with his master for a short beer. The bartender ridiculed the man's claim that his dog could talk.

At this point, the master asked his dog the word for the top of a person's mouth. "Roof," replied the dog. Again the bartender scoffed.

"Okay," said the man. "Watch this." He asked the dog for the word used to describe the covering of a house.

"Roof," the dog again replied.

This was too much for the bartender who walked away in disgust. However, the man followed and pleaded for one more chance. The bartender agreed but added if the dog still refused to talk he would throw out both dog and master.

"Who's the greatest baseball player of all time?" asked the man.

"Roof," barked the dog for the third time as bartender ran both out into the street.

Outside, the master picked himself up and glared down at the dog. The dog glared up at his master and said, "Maybe I should have said Ty Cobb?"

Fresco Thompson has proved himself a brainy man with the Los Angeles Dodgers office. Around the baseball diamond Thompson was always known as a brainy guy with a trigger wit. Once a rookie complained about a slump to Fresco, who asked the youngster how much he was missing the ball by. The rookie measured about a half-inch with thumb and forefinger and Thompson nodded, asking, "Are you hitting over the ball or under the ball?"

"Under it," replied the newcomer. "That's okay, son," said Thompson slapping the kid on the back. "We'll just put some inner-soles in your shoes."

Old Jake Ruppert, 'tis said, is a man who knew how to squelch a bore. At a baseball meeting Ruppert was bothered by a Texan who had worked his way to a position as president of a minor-league team. The talkative Texan wearied everybody with his success story and on this evening he was bending the tired ear of Colonel Jake.

Bragging about his meteoric career and his terrific small-town club, the Texan ended his declaration with a comment about his mounting fortune now approaching the quarter-million dollar mark.

"Fine," yawned multi-millionaire Ruppert. "I'll match you for it."

Pepper Martin was one of the guys who made the old gashouse gang of St. Louis such a star attraction. As dashing as the Cards were on the field, they were equally boisterous off the diamond. Two of the biggest cards on the Cards were Pepper Martin and Dizzy Dean who often painted the town red away from the Stadium.

Observers swear to the story about how Pep and Diz decked themselves out as house painters and broke up a political rally. Carrying their brushes, pails and ladders, the clowning Cards elbowed their way into one of the city's finest restaurants and at the height of the dinner hour they ordered the place vacated so they could start swabbing the walls with paint.

As guests began to scoot in all directions to get clear of Pepper's brush, the manager charged the pair and tossed both Martin and Dean out of the place. However a number of guests were still not convinced so they followed the crazy Cards out into the cool air of the evening.

Among the ranks of baseball announcers there exist a number of 14-karat characters. One of these, as everybody knows, is Dizzy Dean and another is Rosey Rosewell who handles mike chores for the Pittsburgh Pirates. Rosey uses a fictional character name of Aunt Minnie who supposedly occupies a house outside of Forbes Field.

Every time Kiner or Co. lines a home run out of the park, Rosey goes into a tantrum shouting for Aunt Minnie to open the window and save the pane! Once in a while Rosey will smash a piece of glass and scold Aunt Minnie for not opening her window. Rosey is probably one of the most sought-for public speakers in the land because of his wonderful sense of humor.

Jimmy Dykes was always good for a laugh or two during his term as manager of the Chicago White Sox. Once a visitor to the Chicago dressing room saw scrappy James getting a massage by the team trainer and asked if Jimmy expected to play that afternoon.

"Of course not," Jimmy replied. "But what happens when I run up the plate this afternoon and argue with the umpire? You don't want me to fall flat on my face, do you?"

The story is told about the manager who registered a slow burn when he saw a young pitcher uncork a couple of wild pitches. "Don't you think we should take him out?" asked the manager's assistant, innocently.

"We either take him out," replied the sizzling skip-

per with some sarcasm, "or we take out our centerfielder and put in two catchers!"

Baseball managers are usually sticklers on having
their signals obeyed. Quite a few seasons back when
John McGraw was managing the Giants he gave the
bunt signal to his famous pinch-hitter Moose Mc-
Cormick but the Moose saw a cripple crawling up to
the plate so he socked the ball for a solid triple.

As soon as the inning ended, Moose rushed eagerly
to his manager and exclaimed, "How about that
triple!"

"How about that triple!" McGraw blew up. "I told
you to bunt, so that three-bagger will cost you exactly
$50!"

Moose McCormick paid the fine, too.

Ever wonder how that piece of the ballpark used
to warm up relief pitchers came to be called the bullpen? A good many theories have been advanced but
one in particular seems to suggest considerable logic.
It is the explanation that the bullpen is the sort of
place used to fatten up pitchers for the kill before
leading them to be slaughtered on the mound.

Henry Morgan, the well-known radio and television comedian, is a rabid Giant rooter who has an
interesting comment to make on the seating arrange-
ments of ballparks in general. Says Henry, "The only
difference in watching baseball from the bleachers is
that the game is played backwards."

The year after Bucky Harris won a pennant and a
World Series for the Yankees he got the gate. Nevertheless the Yankees gave Bucky a big, fat bonus al-

though he did not win the flag. As some wiseacre observed, "This is probably the first time in baseball history a manager was paid a bonus for not winning a pennant!"

Everybody knows Babe Ruth was a guy who called everybody kiddo and never could remember a name, often after playing several seasons with a chap. Well, Connie Mack and Yogi Berra should go down in baseball history as two of the greatest name-manglers in the game. Take any name in the box-score and chances are both Connie and Yogi will come up with versions different from the correct one.

With Connie, Lou Boudreau is "Lou Boordoo." However, with Yogi Berra, Lou Boudreau comes out "Lou Burdow."

It's only fitting that a chapter on humor in baseball should be ended with something about Casey Stengel. In the days when Casey managed the bottom-of-the-barrel Braves he rarely came across a hot prospect although he tried out hundreds of hopefuls. One afternoon somebody approached tired Stengel and asked about a rookie whom he had turned down in the morning. "How did the boy field?"

"Pretty good fielder," replied Casey.

"Could he hit?" was the next question tossed at Stengel.

"He couldn't hit the ground if he fell out of an airplane," replied Casey Stengel.

Brainy or Balmy

Managers still use as a lesson for young pitchers the maneuver engineered by crafty Miller Huggins back in 1914, the year the "Hitless Wonder" Boston Braves went from last place in mid-season to a pennant and victory in the World Series. The Dodgers, natch, were playing at old League Park in St. Louis and with young Brook chucker Ed Appleton holding his own in a 1-1 duel, Huggins, the Cardinal manager, became desperate for a badly needed win.

"Hey, Appleton," Huggins yelled from his third-base coaching position. "I want to see that baseball you're holding. Throw it over here a minute, will you?"

Innocently, the Dodger kid hurler obliged. Neatly, Huggins stepped aside and allowed the ball to roll all the way to the stands. While every mouth in the ball park hung open, the winning Cardinal run raced in from third. Though the Dodgers protested bitterly, the move was ruled strictly within bounds since nobody had bothered to call time.

Just the same, for every display of brains in baseball there are literally a hundred instances of unsound judgment. Under pressure, it may be conceded, wrong moves are made with ease, although carefully planned procedures have been known to backfire, too.

In case you've ever wondered how Dizzy Trout, Detroit Tiger pitcher, earned his nickname, here is the story. Tiring of shagging flies in the outfield, Trout decided to dash under an awning and shield himself from the sun for awhile. As he reached the awning, Dizzy bounced to the ground, out cold as an ice cube. His teammates revived Diz and explained to him that this awning was not real—was only painted on the left field wall! From that day Paul Trout became Dizzy.

During the pennant stretch of the 1950 National League season, brainy Eddie Stanky raised havoc with Andy Seminick, Philadelphia catcher, with his disturbing antics around second base. Every time the roaring Russian stepped into the batter's box, Stanky would place himself in line with the batter's vision and go into a wild tactic of stretching and waving his arms windmill fashion.

Seminick fussed and fumed and complained violently to the umpires. At one point, angry Andy became so incensed he almost sent the entire Giant infield to the hospital with his bull-like behavior on the basepaths. Finally, to save the Giants from self-invited destruction, the National League's offices ruled against Eddie Stanky's brainstorm and told him to cut out the action, labelled "bush-league stuff" by most sports writers.

During the days Arthur Vance was dazzling them in Brooklyn as Dazzy Vance, fireball pitcher de luxe, he hit upon a snazzy stunt to baffle the batter even further. Taking scissors in hand, Dazzy cut the sleeve of his pitching-arm sweatshirt so the ribbons would flop in the air as he delivered the ball.

Opposing batters went goggle-eyed trying to pick out the pill-like pellet Vance dished up to the plate from among the maze of white created by his sweat-shirt sleeve. Hitters cried like mad against Dazzy's practice but the old fox got away with it for some time. In addition to employing tattered shirtsleeves, pitchers have tried to blind batters with glittering buttons on the cap, shirtfront or glove.

The 1926 World Series saw Babe Ruth do some fancy fence-busting to set a number of batting marks as was the Babe's wont. Yet, truth to tell, the Bambino could easily be termed the goat of that Fall Classic. In the final struggle of the seven-game set the Cards behind old Pete Alexander held a jittery 3-2 lead over the Yanks. New York hearts took a leap late in the game, as invincible Alex walked Ruth on a close three-and-two pitch.

Thus, the Yanks had a life and things took on an even rosier hue as bustling Bob Meusel stepped in to take his cuts against the tiring reliever, old man Alexander, who had just worked a full game the day before. Then, for some unexplained reason, and while thousands stared in disbelief, the roly poly Babe set sail for second base with Alex working on Meusel at the plate.

The story goes that Babe had decided to steal second base on his own; he had picked up no signal to do so from any coach. Of course it was easy as pie for the Card catcher of the day to peg down to Rogers Hornsby at second for the tag on Ruth and an upset Series victory for the under-rated St. Louis club.

On August 4, 1945, there occurred in Boston the

strangest stolen base possibly on record. The Dodgers were visiting the Braves and pint-sized Vic Lombardi was working on the mound for the Brooks. The little lefty walked shortstop Dick Culler but with catcher Phil Masi at the plate, Lombardi trapped Culler off first base.

Immediately Boston coach Benny Bengough shouted "Balk!" Umpire Magerkurth nodded and pointed to second as Culler waltzed over to the keystone sack. At this point it developed the only one in the ball park to call a balk had been quick-thinking coach Bengough.

As Dodger second-sacker Eddie Stanky tossed cap, ball and glove into left field in a white rage, Culler was allowed to remain at second because time out had not been called officially. Sympathizing with Stanky, the umpires overlooked his petulant performance and allowed him to remain in the game. As so often happens in such cases, Culler came home with the deciding run as big Bill Lee blanked the Dodgers.

Bob Elliott, long an All-Star third-baseman for the Pittsburgh Pirates and for the Boston Braves, was a player who used his head as well as his bat. On fly balls to the outfield, Elliott keeps pointing to the base runner's feet, keeping him glued to third base until the ball is positively caught. Bob's method works so effectively, he sometimes delays a runner long enough for the outfielder to peg him out at home plate.

Baseball owners will go to any lengths—except sometimes spend heavy money—to improve the chances of their respective teams. At the start of the 1950 season, for example, the St. Louis Browns management figured they would instill the winning spirit in their charges by hiring a psychiatrist to convince the cellar dwellers they weren't really that bad.

The mind man worked hard but his results are open to conjecture. Conceded, the Browns had the winning spirit, they nevertheless had a losing team. And it's probably not true, as some wags would have you believe, that the Browns eventually drove the psychiatrist out of his mind.

Perhaps the Browns got the idea of hiring a man of medicine from their city brothers—the Cards—of ten years previous. That was the season the St. Louis Gas-House Gang made headlines by feeding vitamin B-1 tablets to the ball players and the Cardinals apparently did right well with this new-found strength, finishing second to the Dodgers only after a red-hot pennant battle. Since this represented an advance of one notch over 1940, naturally vitamin tablets could not be blamed for any adverse action.

You have to go a long way to locate a more trigger-thinker than Mike (King) Kelly of the old Boston 1899 club. Although Kelly was warming the bench on this fine day, his agile brain was working like mad. As a Cincinnati batter lofted a foul fly in the direction of the Boston dugout it became evident to Kelly that his own catcher would never be able to reach the ball.

Quick as lightning, Kelly was on his feet. "Kelly now catching for Boston," he roared, making the substitution official in keeping with the rules of the day. Then King Kelly quietly reached forward and caught the ball for an all-important out. Later, the regulations on substitutions were changed but in catcher

Kelly's times his snappy substituting was completely legal.

If you think intelligence has no place in the makeup of a major-league baseball player, think again. Dumb bunnies with plenty of raw strength have a way of fading from the big time while less talented but more quick-thinking performers seem to make the important lineups year after year.

For evidence weigh well the wise words of George Susce, uttered when George managed the Batavia, New York club of the Class D Pony League. It was George's job to try out newcomers to baseball and when he described a certain infielder, listeners believed George to have discovered a genuine star on the horizon.

"The kid had everything," George declared. "Fast, strong, with big hands and he could really peg that baseball across the diamond. Too bad he'll never make good in the majors."

The gathering could not believe its ears. "How come a guy with such ability can't make good in the majors?" somebody asked.

"His IQ wasn't high enough," George answered solemnly.

Smart pitchers are accepted as good pitchers and Howie Pollet, star Cardinal portsider for many years, is no exception. An honor student at high school, majoring in English, philosophy, and psychology, high-flying Howie invested his first big-league paycheck in a set of the Harvard Classics. In fact, Howie's life-long ambition has been to become a college professor.

Almost as old as baseball is the hidden-ball trick.

What with time-outs and the sharp eyes of coaches along the baselines, it has become extremely difficult for a major-league infielder to conceal the ball and put the tag on an unsuspecting baserunner leaving his bag for the customary lead. Frankie Crosetti was perhaps the last big-leaguer to practice the stunt with any degree of success, although Tony Cuccinello was also pretty good at it a number of seasons back.

Crosetti learned the art from later-day umpire Babe Pinelli when both were playing at San Francisco, Frankie as a rookie and Babe as a veteran. To get the gimmick under way, Pinelli would walk over to the pitcher's mound tossing the ball into the air and catching it as he went. Instead of handing the pitcher the ball, however, Babe would quite cutely drop it unobserved into his mitt. From that point on it actually was no trick at all for Pinelli to tag out the inattentive runner.

Today such a system would be difficult indeed. Now before the pitcher can step on the rubber he must have possession of the ball. The crafty runner will wait until the pitcher makes such a move to avoid being caught off base via the hidden-ball trick.

Conversation is an important factor in trapping any runner off base. Crossetti used the chatter approach to perfection, almost, engaging rival base runners in harmless conversation until an unsuspecting one would absently step off the base. That would be enough of a slip for Crossetti to tag the poor chap out. Oscar Melillo was another conversationalist who specialized in hidden-ball antics, and successfully!

Not so long ago Tony Cuccinnello worked the hidden-ball trick against the Cleveland Indians while Cooch was holding down a war-time third base for the Chicago White Sox. In the last half of the 13th of a tie game, Indian skipper Lou Boudreau started activities with a resounding three-base smack.

No sooner did Lou pull up at third, than he stepped off to discover, horrified, that he was the victim of a Cuccinello hidden ball. Naturally, the fans gave Boudreau a rousing razzing, for of all people the manager should never be guilty of such a mental lapse.

Today the hidden-ball trick seems like an art lost but some cagey manager may yet be able to circumvent the rules enough to revive baseball's most embarrassing play.

Anybody who has seen big John Mize step to the plate as one of the National League's all-time slugging greats never could help but wonder how Georgia Jawn was able to handle so heavy a bat with such an amount of ease. John twirled the big bat around his shoulders like a toothpick and sent the ball spinning as deeply into the stands as any slugger in history.

Well, the gracious if not graceful first-baseman had a system all his own. Big John always kept three bats on hand, one weighing 35 ounces, one 34, and one 33. "First time up," admitted John, "I feel real strong so I use the 35 ouncer, next time the 34 and then the 33." Sound logic and, judging by the amount of round-trippers banged by muscular Mize, a sound system.

It was the opening game of the 1929 World Series and Connie Mack rocked the baseball world to its very heels by starting against the rough-tough Cubs a pitcher named Howard Ehmke, an aging veteran who had appeared in only a few games during the course of the regular season and then mostly in relief. "Is Connie crazy?" asked every sage of the age.

For the Cubs it was their first World Series since 1910 and more than anything else in the world they wanted to win this one. Gleefully, they watched Ehmke warm up and they figured they would treat his slow stuff like batting practice serves. Here was Ehmke who had pitched a total of 55 innings during the regular season, including only two complete games. Not only did Ehmke set down the Cubs by a 3-1 count and limit the little bears to eight hits, but he fanned 13 of the Chicagoans, erasing a strike-out record of 12 held by Ed Walsh ever since 1906.

The wise man of baseball, Connie Mack, almost added insult to the well-known injury by bringing back Ehmke to pitch the fifth and final game of the Series. Once again, Howard did quite well by himself but left the game trailing by a 2-0 count as Cub chucker Pat Malone did even better. Going into the bottom of the ninth, Malone had a two-hit shutout only to see the amazing A's explode for three big runs and the ball game, wrapping up the Series for the American League, four games to one.

Had Ehmke remained in the game it is not beyond belief that Howie would have won the first and last games of the classic. At that, though, Mr. Mack showed a good deal of solid judgment in pulling one of baseball's biggest coups de guerre. As a matter of fact, Eddie Sawyer, manager of the pennant-winning 1950 Philadelphia nine, almost pulled another Mack-Ehmke by starting his star relief hurler, Jim Konstanty, in the first game of the 1950 Series. Like Ehmke, Konstanty pitched a whale of a game but ultimately bowed to the superior hurling ability of the Series-winning New York Yankee mound staff.

One of baseball's all-time great relief pitchers was of course Wilcy Moore, pride of the Yankee bullpen back in the late 1920's. Stuff, Wilcy is not said to have had much of; brains he possessed a-plenty, insist the wiseacres of the diamond. Those who observed him best claim Wilcy knew the batting weakness of every hitter in the American League and what's more, Wilcy was able to pitch to the weakness with his soft-looking stuff. The combination of control and brains, in fact, seems to be the factor that makes any reliever great.

After Wilcy's great 1927 season with the Yankees when he won 19 and lost 7, mostly in relief, and sported the lowest earned run average in the league, his arm went dead and he drifted back to the minors. His biggest critics called Moore's success in the majors a one-year fluke and they appeared to be correct until he bobbed up with St. Paul of the American Association.

Here, in 1930, Wilcy Moore once again called on the big brain to rack up 22 wins while dropping nine and fanning 101 batsmen. The Moore prowess was well recognized around the league and the Milwaukee Journal once ran a headline reading, "Good news for the Brewers, Moore Won't Pitch Today."

And Wilcy did come back to the majors to astound further the disbelievers. After a so-so season with the pennant-powerhouse Yanks of 1932, Wilcy came on to show his stuff in the World Series against the Chicago Cubs. The Yanks swept the Series in four and Wilcy made his mound appearance in the final contest, relieving Johnny Allen who had been battered by the Cubs for four runs in the first inning.

With two away, Wilcy Moore took over from Allen and put out the fire. Between the first and sixth innings when he retired for a pinch-hitter, Moore called upon his cunning to limit the Chicago pack to one lone run on two stingy hits. Although Herb Pennock worked the last two innings and the New Yorkers atomized the Cubs 13-6, Wilcy Moore was adjudged the winning pitcher!

Wee Willie Keeler, the mythical place-hitter of long ago, was a man of brains. Playing with the New York Americans of 1903, Keeler found himself on third base with a chap, name of Ganzel, on second. On a grounder to short, Willie tried to score but the Washington shortstop had him out by a mile so Willie pulled up short, grinned and stuck out his hand to congratulate Washington catcher Kittredge on the heads-up play.

Naturally the rival catcher was flattered to pieces by Willie's gesture. As he modestly accepted Keeler's praise, Kittredge almost swallowed the ball when the Wee One dashed past him to the plate. In great haste, the desperate catcher uncorked a throw to his pitcher covering home, but the hasty peg hit Willie smack in the back and rolled to the stands. As a result of Willie's brainy maneuver, Ganzel also came loping in to score all the way from second.

Take it from one of baseball's keenest students of the game, Muddy Ruel, baseball is not putting nearly enough emphasis on the thinking points of the game. Muddy is a guy who should know whereof he speaks, having served for many years as coach for the White Sox and Indians and as manager of the St. Louis Browns.

According to Muddy, the mass production of baseball's farm systems often overlooks the player as an individual and frequently brings him to the majors before he is ready. It is Ruel's opinion that rookies today know less than they did a dozen years ago. He thinks it is wrong for scouts to insist exclusively on height and brawn in the hitters and speed in a pitcher.

"Slow-balling Gene Beardon of the 1948 pennant-winning Indians became Rookie of the Year, didn't he?" offers Muddy Ruel in argument.

Ty Cobb has often been noted for his daring, brainy base-running but he too goes down in baseball lore as one of those who tried to steal a base already occupied by a teammate. The Georgia Peach pulled the boner—one of his few—in a game against Washington in 1915. Hell-bent for third, Cobb suddenly pulled up short when he saw fellow Tiger, Donnie Bush, on the bag. When Cobb tried in vain to get back to second he was called out. Cobb objected to the decision violently, so Umpire Rhody Wallace put him out again, this time out of the game!

The Philadelphia Phillies of 1950 almost sold their first pennant in 35 years down the river before the season officially got under way. Convinced that catcher Andy Seminick had passed his peak, the Phils put the big Russian on the block and had a deal all set—Seminick for catcher Clyde McCullough and infielder

Pete Castiglione of the Pirates. However, the deal fell through and lucky for the Phils as Anvil Andy was a big man in the Quaker City pennant drive.

Frankie Frisch, probably baseball's most colorful manager of his day, figures batting practice is just a waste of time. "What good is it?" Frankie asks. "A .320 hitter steps up and takes a couple of swings—and goes on hitting .320. A .260 hitter practices and practices—and goes on hitting .260. Frankie Frisch concludes that batting licks are just one big waste of time and energy.

Temperamental Tidbits

An uneven temper, some say, is the mark of an unsteady ball player. This may be more fiction than truth though. Present-day popoff guys such as Don Drysdale of the Dodgers or the Yankee superstar, Mickey Mantle, are certainly better than average. And who can find better men with the bat than four of the most temperamental men you could name in the history of the game: Babe Ruth, Ty Cobb, Rogers Hornsby and Ted Williams.

In former days, as now, pitchers have always contributed their share of temperament to the game. Former Yankee Johnny Allen used to toss his glove high in the air over any umpire's call to which he took exception. Van Mungo of the Dodgers never hesitated to point an accusing finger at an erring infielder. Dizzy Dean had his moments. Don Newcombe was another who used to blow sky high when things weren't going his way. In fact, it is the rare baseball player who has not gotten excited at one time or another. Even that great shortstop and gentleman, Pee Wee Reese of the Dodgers, a most mild-mannered Kentucky Colonel, got himself thrown out of a game. Mickey Mantle's violent temper has been seen on more than one occasion. After a particularly unfortunate strikeout, Mantle, in great disgust, formed a habit of furiously kicking the water cooler in the Yankee dugout. Even the wealthy Yanks became annoyed about the frequency of the repair bill.

Probably one of the all-time temperamental men of the mound was the immortal Lefty Grove, officially listed as Robert Moses Grove. It was in St. Louis against the Browns that Lefty was working like mad to down the lowly St. Louis gang and become the first American League pitcher in history to chalk up 17 straight wins. Lefty lost the game 1-0 to Dick Coffman, usually not so effective, and old man Mose dropped the heart-breaking squeaker because rookie outfielder Jim Moore misjudged a fly ball.

The oddity about the whole episode is that the fiery fireballer did not explode over his outfielder's error in execution. To the amazement of everyone on his bench, Lefty Grove took the loss in stride. But later that same afternoon he did get hot under the sweatshirt because in the second game of the doubleheader, his mates who could not scrape together one lone run for Lefty Grove got ten markers for Waite Hoyt!

As manager of the Hollywood Club in the Pacific Coast League, Jimmy Dykes was always an explosive and colorful character. There was the time infielder Billy Schuster pulled the hidden-ball trick on one of Dykes' baserunners. Naturally, cigar-smoking Jimmy blew his stack.

As a lesson in attention, manager Dykes fined both coaches. One was Harry Danning. The other? Jimmy Dykes!

One of the most gentlemanly men known to baseball was Pie Traynor, Pittsburgh's all-time number one third-baseman. Never did a cussword cross the lips of Pie and only once in his career was the silent

one ever chased from a ball game. The incident occurred at the hands of Mr. Baseball Umpire himself,
Bill Klem, and the grand old grouch never could forget the circumstances.

Out of a clear blue sky Pie walked up to Klem,
looked the ancient arbiter squarely in the eyes, and
said in an even but firm voice, "I'm getting sick and
tired of your silly decisions." For Pie Traynor, that
was explosive!

Like many great performers, Rogers Hornsby was
given to displays of temperament. Throughout his
final days as a Cardinal, the mighty Rogers found it
increasingly difficult to sit on the same bench with
his manager, Branch Rickey. It is said Rogers and
Branch actually came to blows under the stands at
Sportsman's Park on one occasion and on another
later in the same season, 1923, Branch and Sam
Breadon fined Hornsby $500 and suspended him for
refusing to play. Hornsby gave as his alibi a skin ailment which he said hampered his movement tremen-
dously. The management and Hornsby were still at a
Mexican standoff when the curtain closed down the
season.

In spite of such complaints, Rogers Hornsby was
all ball player. One year later, in 1924, he came slash-
ing back to hit .424, all-time modern major-league
high, and he established this figure with a lifeless sixth
place team!

One of the stormiest of careers was experienced by
Hal Chase who operated under a cloud of suspicion
during one period of his major-league tenure. There

are many who contend Hal Chase was the best first-baseman ever known to baseball, a guy who could have been even better had he so desired.

Chase was a sort of happy-go-lucky but ornery character in his way. His teammates disliked him and when he became manager of the old New York Yankees nobody would play for him. He had a habit of criticizing his own infielders and they really tried to make him look bad on occasion by deliberately throwing poorly to first base. Hal Chase scooped up everything in sight anyway.

Throughout his many terms under the big top, Hal Chase drifted from one club to another and finally he disappeared from baseball completely, just like that. Nobody could find a trace of the great Chase. No club wanted him and nobody tried too hard to locate him. Then came news of his death and a portion of Hal Chase's life was just blotted out.

About the last time Hal Chase's name figured prominently in major-league baseball was back during the days of the White Sox-Black Sox scandal. Already eased out as an active player because of questionable conduct, Hal popped into the picture as one of the boys to put the fix on the World Series. That marked the bitter end in baseball for extremely capable Hal Chase.

One of baseball's milder minds had always been Hall-of-Famer Mel Ott, the great little New York Giant and home-run king of the National League. Ottie was always an easy guy to get along with until he took to managing, and ill temper under such conditions can usually be excused.

Most memorable blowup by mighty Melvin concerned his ace pitcher, Big Bill Voiselle. Willy had
been a hot potato for the stumbling Jints of the day,
piling up 21 wins in 1944. In 1945 Bill continued his
winning ways by taking six straight at one point.

Then at Sportsman's Park, St. Louis, the Giants held
a slim 1-0 lead over the Cards going into the bottom
of the last inning. Bill Voiselle, on the mound for the
visitors, seemed to have the situation in hand although
a Red Bird roosted on base and damaging Johnny
Hopp waved a wicked willow at the plate. Quickly,
Voiselle put across two straight strikes. He came down
with his third pitch and Hopp wallopped it for a
triple, scoring the tying run. Eventually Hopp made
his way home from third with the winning marker and
manager Mel Ott was obviously displeased with the
outcome.

Melvin the manager sought out Voiselle in the clubhouse. "What's the big idea of throwing a strike with
two strikes and no balls on the batter?" thundered
Ott at his big pitcher. "That will cost you five hundred bucks!"

Eventually cooling off, Ott withdrew the fine but
the criticism had hurt Voiselle, affected his work on
the mound. He no longer became the big winner and
his attitude toward the Giant manager brought about
his disposal to the Boston Braves. Temperament, in
this case, did the Giants no good at all.

Back in the days when Ty Cobb was stealing bases
like a canvas kleptomaniac, he probably made almost
as many enemies as Adolf Hitler. Infielders on every
opposing team resented the way Ty came tearing into

them, spikes flying, and hell-bent on only one thing: a successful steal.

Eddie Collins, mild-mannered as anybody in baseball, joined those who feuded with the Georgia Peach. It was Eddie's determination to put the tag on Ty squarely between the eyes if the sack-stealer ever cut him down at his position. However, try as he might, Eddie could never carry out the threat, as Cobb had a way of evading such retaliatory methods as he uncorked his vicious and tricky slide. Cobb got his medicine on occasion but he always dished it out in larger quantities than he took.

Ty took no abuse from anyone. As he was carving his enviable niche in baseball's archives, Ty gave vent to such an outburst of temper at one point, he drew an indefinite suspension from the American League. With his action he almost broke up the Detroit Tigers.

During a Detroit visit to New York, Cobb became incensed at the behavior of a local fan who heckled him, finally jumping the railing and taking a few solid punches at the offender. Umpires and players rushed to the fan's rescue and Ty Cobb promptly was expelled from the game.

The Tigers without Cobb were like tigers without claws and the players pulled a startling move by going on strike in an effort to have the Georgia Peach reinstated. The Detroit management would have none of this action, so the front office fielded a team made up mostly of semi-pros and semi-retired athletes. Naturally the old guys got their collective heads handed to them in their first encounter. With Cobb's backing, the league offices persuaded the regular

Tigers to play again and as a sort of concession lifted the suspension in about a dozen quick days.

Umpire Bill Klem knew how to handle temperamental ball players. In fact, he incorporated his methods into a handbook of instruction for umpires in the National League. One part reads: "If a player should become overly belligerent, say, 'Are you a fighter, too? I thought you were a ball player'." Klem claims the treatment always worked for him.

Like everybody else in the business world, ball players sometimes change their minds from day to day. Babe Herman tells a hilarious story on Butch Henline, well-regarded National League umpire who played with the Daffy Dodgers of the Herman era.

Henline had long been sulking about his unproductive position on the bench when he longed to be behind the plate working in a few games as Dodger catcher. In desperation, Henline finally appealed to Babe Herman to put in a good word for Butch with manager Wilbert Robinson. The good-natured Babe did and Butch was donning the mask and mitt pronto.

For one, two, three, four, five games straight Butch Henline caught for the Dodgers. On the sixth day Henline again came complaining to Babe Herman. "What is this, Babe?" he asked. "Are they going to make me catch every game from now until the end of the season?"

The temperament of Ted Williams has always been a matter of conversation. Always an outspoken guy, Ted's actions are the same on any field including his own backyard, Fenway Park up in Boston, where he once gestured with his hands in ungentlemanly fashion as a means of telling the fans to go jump in the lake.

Even during his wartime service days, Ted did a bit of first-class exploding. It occurred at Pearl Harbor where a Navy World Series was in progress. After popping up in a crucial moment, tall Ted became so angry he tossed his bat high in the air and if Dick Wakefield hadn't deflected the lumber it would have hit a Navy photographer hard on top of the head.

The spectators of course booed Williams for his action and this didn't set well with the Splendid Splinter at all. So he promptly drew back his foot and gave the photographer's equipment a good, solid boot that sent the stuff flying in all directions!

Some of Babe Ruth's color was attributed to his often uncontrollable temper. The big boy would pop off at one time and behave like a prince at another. All in all, the Bambino was a rather unpredictable person.

After the 1931 season, Babe Ruth was threatened with a $5,000 cut from his $80,000. These were depression times and Babe had not been at his best during 1931 either. A group of sports writers were discussing the slash with the Babe and ribbing him a bit when one said, "Don't forget, Babe, at $75,000 you'll still be making as much as President Hoover."

The Babe accepted the comment philosophically. "Well, Hoover had a bad year too, didn't he?"

One of baseball's biggest popoffs was also one of the game's most talented performers: Rogers Hornsby. Poor Rogers just couldn't keep quiet during his playing days in the big time and as a result he was always earning unfavorable newspaper publicity.

During his very first term as a major-league manager, the great Rajah got into an argument with a rival, Arthur Fletcher, and flattened him with a single punch. Usually, Rogers never resorted to force; he just argued, and argued, and argued until he became a source of annoyance to even his teammates.

Rarely, however, did Hornsby argue with the umpires. He was too smart for that. He did on one occasion and precipitated a riot. In the twilight of a wonderful career, Hornsby was playing with the Braves against his old Cardinal teamsters. Rogers' altercation with the arbiter brought the fans flowing on the field, waving pop bottles in his defense. Order was restored and Rogers Hornsby drew a five-day suspension for bringing about a riot.

George Metkovich is a hard-swatting ballplayer who has been up and down between the majors and minors on a number of occasions. George was always one of those minor-league flashes who just don't seem to stick in the majors.

Take the 1950 season for example which saw George become the most valuable player in the Pacific Coast League. Naturally he was drafted for another try at the big time and the man to do the drafting was Mahatma Branch Rickey.

This time Metkovich balked. He didn't want to go to the majors, he insisted. He liked it in the Coast League with Oakland where he could get in his licks every day instead of warming a big-league bench. George had bought himself a home in Long Beach and his kids were attending school there. The guy who was good enough to get a third try at big-league baseball waged a one-man war to stay away from the big time, unbelievable as it may seem! But he came up again to finish his big league career with Milwaukee.

Both on the field and off, the life of Enos (Country) Slaughter, star St. Louis Cardinal outfielder, has been marked with tumult. The first two marriages of Slaughter ended in the divorce courts and on the field Slaughter has had his share of flareups. One concerned the spiking in the heel of Jackie Robinson, when the Negro star was breaking in with the Brooklyn Dodgers as a full-time first-baseman. It isn't that Country Slaughter seeks trouble; he just plays the game to the hilt, no matter what the consequences.

You take a screwball character like Bobo Newsome and you wonder sometimes why a guy should carry on like that. Well, in Bobo's own words—as told to an AP reporter—there was always a method to his madness.

Newsome related the incident of a chat he had with another big-league pitcher who scolded him a bit for his lack of finesse on the mound. "Why don't you cut out the showboat stuff, Bobo," advised this other pitcher.

So Newsome asked the guy how many games he had won the previous season. It developed the other pitcher had notched twice as many victories as did Bobo. Then Bobo inquired as to the guy's salary.

"You see," pointed out Bobo, "color counts. Last year you won twice as many games as I did, yet I earned twice as much money!"

A milder, nicer guy than Dixie Walker never lived; on the other hand, a more violent ball player than

Ben Chapman never donned a pair of spikes. It was Chapman, who as Philadelphia manager, in later years drew censure from the National League offices for jockeying rookie Jackie Robinson of the Brooks to a degree beyond endurance.

Yet quiet Dixie and boisterous Ben Chapman were cast together with the great New York Yankees as brother outfielders, Chapman a regular and Dixie a sub. It was odd, too, that they should both almost wind up in jail during a Yankee visit to the Washington ball park.

On a close play at second, hard-running Ben Chapman hit into Senator second-sacker Buddy Myer so hard he bowled over the plucky Nat. They fought in the dust and they fought on their feet after players separated them. Quickly the umpires restored order by banishing both to the showers. To reach the clubhouse Chapman had to pass through the Washington ball players, eventually swinging a haymaker at pitcher Earl Whitehill.

Almost immediately the entire Washington bench jumped Ben, spectators leaving their seats to get in a sock at the unpopular outfielder. Poor Chapman was taking his medicine alone until a nearby teammate, lanky Dixie Walker, jumped to his assistance. Pretty soon all the Yankees were there but the cops pulled out Chapman and Walker as instigators of the riot and both were bundled off in the direction of the clink. To make sure no repetition occurred, the men in blue marched Dixie and Ben clear to the train station where they were whisked off to Philadelphia.

For Ben Chapman, such goings-on were not unusual; for Dixie Walker, they were unbelievable.

Tinker to Evers to Chance has become a lasting baseball phrase, indicating the ace ability of the Cub infield to rattle off double-plays during the early years of the 20th century. From 1906 to 1910, Tinker to Evers to Chance played a major role in bringing four pennants to the Chicago Cub ball park.

Although Tinker to Evers to Chance exemplified smooth action on the diamond's infield, they were anything but in their relations to one another. It's a matter of record that the thrilling threesome hated one another, yet their mutual hate was buried by their will to win.

Johnny Evers and Joe Tinker were not on speaking terms although working well enough on the twin-killing to win two pennants. Can anyone imagine such a startling situation? It was almost a common oc-currence for Tinker and Evers to resort to physical violence in the clubhouse. Frank Chance, though hav-ing no real love for either, usually broke up the fight.

Chance was manager of that club and as leader he had to keep the boys from each other's throats. In 1912 the great combination was broken up and it is a tribute to their all-around cooperative ability that their names are very familiar to baseball fans of this generation.

Baseball's Blackest Bits

The story of the abortive Black Sox episode is familiar to every baseball fan. But baseball has experienced other scandals. In fact, one of its earliest almost wrecked the game before it started. Scandal number one occurred only two brief years after the National League became a body and the body was almost embalmed and buried in the year 1877 to be precise. To make the calamity even greater, the scandal involved one of the greatest pitchers of the era, Jim Devlin, ranking right alongside the renowned A.G. Spalding as Mr. Big of the pitching mound in those days.

The nation was rocked to its post-Civil War heels by the charge that four members of the Louisville team, A. H. Nichols, George Hall, W. H. Draver and Jim Devlin were bobbling games to the Hartford team for a cash consideration in the neighborhood of colossal $100. Oddly enough, the first big scandal, coming immediately after the War between the States, paralleled baseball's next important shocker in 1919 involving the Black Sox and taking place about a year after World War I.

League president William A. Hulbert of 1877 acted swiftly and surely, nipping the plot in the baseball bud by forcing three of the players to turn over telegrams exchanged between the Louisville players and gamblers which showed strong evidence of collusion. When he refused to produce his telegram, Craven, the fourth plotter, was kicked out of baseball at once. Hall and Devlin came through with confessions. Although influential followers of the sport pleaded for clemency, league headquarters banished the entire quartet forever from the game.

The severe punishment effectively put an end to gambling temptation, a definite threat to baseball in those forgotten days when the paychecks of players were considerably thinner than they are today. Some time later George Hall tried playing semi-pro ball in Jersey under a nom de plume; however, he was discovered and banished a second time.

Back in the days shortly before the Gay Nineties, Charley Comiskey's St. Louis Browns copped the American Association flag and moved into World Series play against Pop Anson's Chicago White Stockings of the National League. Nobody ever won this Fall Classic for it changed from a baseball contest to a slugging match with players on both teams doing their darndest to bash in the heads of the enemy. Scandalous behavior, to be sure!

Both managers, Cap Anson and Charles Comiskey, accused each other of quitting. For that reason record books list the World Series of 1885 as a tie and the incident almost put an end to the Fall Classic.

Curiously, the same teams won pennants in their respective leagues and actually agreed to meet in another World Series—that of 1886—on a winner-take-all wager. And that's the way it was contested with the Browns grabbing the honors, four games to two. As a little side bet, each club put $500 on the line to cover its own players. Can you imagine the scandal such an arrangement would cause in present-day baseball?

The World Series was to experience another tie in 1890, but this time for another reason. Many of the game's most talented performers jumped the big leagues to organize their own loop, the Players League. Although this experiment went flat broke in one season it detracted much attention from organized baseball and created an apathetic attitude toward the 1890 Series. When the Brooklyn Nationals and the Louisville A. A. Colonels won three games each and tied one, both clubs decided to drop the whole thing for nobody was coming out to see them play anyhow. What's more, a premature cold wave had discouraged what rabid fans remained from attending the tilts.

Most athletes returned to their former clubs when the Players League went poof in 1891. Nevertheless, a little underhand manipulation popped into the picture and raiding of rosters developed. The American Association pointed a guilty finger at Pittsburgh, accusing Smoky City execs of pirating a player from the rival league and since those days Pittsburgh has always been known as the Pirates. After much bickering and little dickering between the two leagues, baseball almost came to an organized end until the National League bought out its rival to become only one loop.

Baseball's first modern World Series between American and National League representatives was officially set for the fall of 1903 and then almost didn't come off. Contracts of the Boston American League winners expired in September and the players threatened to be elsewhere for the Series unless they took home a generous slice of the Fall Classic proceeds. At length, for downing the Pittsburgh Pirates in the playoffs, each Boston player earned $1,182, while the club owner drew less than $7,000.

Dineen, ace Boston pitcher, won three games in the 1903 World Series, two by shutouts, while dropping only one contest. In the second game Dineen fanned 11 Pirate batters. For the Pirates, Phillips turned in a curious but effective performance by winning three and losing two. In the first tilt Phillips struck out ten men and then earned the distinction of pitching and winning two complete Series games in a row, the third and fourth contests. However, he was helped by a day's rainfall in between.

St. Louis has had its share of diamond misfortunes. In 1898, fire broke out under the wooden stands of Sportsman's Park and unsuspecting spectators figuring nothing more serious than a fight had developed refused to recognize the frantic warnings from the field of ball players and umpires. The ensuing rush for exits caused many fans to be trampled and burned in the tragedy and brought an overwhelming amount of lawsuits against the club management. Only by selling out were the owners able to keep St. Louis in the league.

Baseball in the '90's was anything but a sissy sport. During that decade, the hustlin' cussin' Cleveland Spiders objected to an ump's decision in Louisville and fists flew as freely as adjectives. The battle spread to such alarming proportions, police ran the entire Spider squad into the hoosegow. Fines were slapped on four Spider stalwarts — captain Pat Tebeau, Ed McClean, Jesse Burkett and Jimmy McAleer — with the National League assessing the aggressive Tebeau an additional $200.

The year was 1926 and again rumors of underhand operations on the diamond were running rampant. Nobody could ignore the accusations and Judge Landis stopped pulling his white hair long enough to summon all of 35 players to a hurried hearing on Swede Risberg's charge that the Detroit Tigers of 1917 had tossed two games to the Chicago White (Black) Sox. Then, before reporters at this open hearing, Landis dramatically weighed the testimony of Risberg and announced the case was closed. "Insufficient evidence," he said.

On another occasion, Landis sent out a hurry call for Ty Cobb and Tris Speaker. Word seeped through to the commissioner's ears that Cobb and Speaker had bet on a fixed game. Both were found innocent as babes in bed. Two New York Giants, Cozy Dolan and Jimmy O'Connell, were cleared similarly in an alleged attempt to fix a game with the Phillies.

Sports and betting are so closely allied, the finger of suspicion is all too often pointed at the innocent by excitable fans. Who can ever forget Umpire George Hildebrand's boner in calling the second game of the 1922 World Series "on account of darkness" while the sun was still beaming down on the playing field? Immediately the hue and cry of fix went up although who could benefit from a 3-3 ten-inning tie is hard to figure. Shawkey of the Yanks and Barnes of the Giants duelled in the sun that afternoon, each permitting eight safeties.

However, Judge Landis was quick to act on Hildebrand's rock. "Play the game over and turn all receipts over to charity," commanded the commissioner. Even with the extra game, the Yanks couldn't win one and the Giants grabbed honors four games to zero. From the second game tie incident on, no World Series game was ever allowed to be called without the consent of the commissioner, although today's use of arc lights has eliminated that possibility.

Before Judge Landis passed on, he waved his iron rule again. This time he bounced from baseball no less a power than Bill Cox, owner of the Philadelphia Phillies. Reason for the high-handed action was the judge's contention he had evidence of the Philly prexy betting on the outcome of a game between the Quakers and another club.

When Jackie Robinson joined the Brooklyn Dodgers in 1947 after a scintillating season at Montreal, fever ran high among some ball players against allowing a Negro to perform in the major leagues. Most publicized event of course was the threatened player strike against the Dodgers by the St. Louis Cardinals during the first swing through the West by the Brooks.

"Pull that strike," National League President Ford Frick is reported to have told the Cardinal delegation, "and you're through in the big leagues." And Frick wasn't fooling. Insiders intimate that Frick called the Cards on his carpet and instructed each and every recalcitrant he would bar him forever from baseball even if such action ruined the class of the senior circuit for a decade.

Unbelievably, the entire abortive action against clean-playing Robbie was reported to be instigated by a member of the Dodger's own team. Who the mystery Dodger was nobody will tell openly, but the finger of suspicion has pointed at different Brook performers from time to time. Dixie Walker has vigorously denied allegations that he threatened to quit the team if Robbie were signed. Those who know the former "People's Choice" best deny Dixie would behave in such unsportsmanlike manner, and in view of Walker's excellent record for fair play it is impossible to decide otherwise.

The Cards weren't the only Cads in Robbie's case. Practically every nine in the majors was gunning for Jackie with Ben Chapman, then manager of the Phillies, most outspoken of the lot. Ben rode Robinson so hard from the bench, mediator Frick had to step in again and advise the MGR to keep his attacks on a more liberal level.

Larry MacPhail was another Jack Robinson opponent in a sort of indirect way. "Serve the Negro in baseball best by letting the Negro leagues carry on in their own fashion," the former Yankee official has been quoted as saying. Somebody else had Dixie Walker saying, "As long as he isn't with the Dodgers yet, I'm not worried." This statement has long since been denied by Dixie. However, thanks to the unrelenting stand taken by National League president Ford Frick, baseball probably survived another scandal in the Jackie Robinson episode.

Maybe his nickname is Stormy, but Roy Weatherly was the only Cleveland Indian of 1940 who did not petition Cleveland prexy J. Alva Bradley for removal of Tribe pilot Oscar Vitt. "Ridiculing players before other members of the team and before sports writers, managerial boners and lack of harmony on the team" were among the beefs levelled by Indians against chief Vitt.

Diplomacy on the part of Cleveland officials squelched the Redskin uprising but it still smacks of a baseball near-scandal, these players shifting the blame of the game to poor Vitt. As it was, Cleveland did not win the 1940 pennant, flubbing the flag by one game to the Detroit Tigers. Then to add scandal to scandal, star third baseman Ken Keltner grabbed horrible headlines by going to his state labor department after the season's end and applying for unemployment insurance!

Came 1941 and the Tribe of Cleveland was still engaged in inter warfare. Now Roger Peckinpaugh sat in the lead wigwam and he too experienced managerial hardships. "No hustle," grumbled Peck in complaint of his athletes whereas during the previous season the shoe had been on the other foot and kicked at the manager. Of all guys, Roy Weatherly turned out to be the villain, Weatherly, the only member to remain loyal to his manager the year before.

On two separate occasions, manager Peckinpaugh publicly accused the squat, hard-hitting outfielder of not giving his all for the Cleveland alma mater. The second time Peck threw up his hands, fined Weatherly $100 and told Roy, "Go home!" According to the manager, Weatherly had not exerted himself in retrieving the ball on a Doc Cramer inside-the-park homer. In no uncertain terms, Roy declared himself through with Cleveland and particularly with manager Roger Peckinpaugh.

However, the larruping lefty was back in Indian livery for 1942 when he appeared in 128 games and hit .258, knocking 39 runs across the platter. Roy in fact had shuttled across the majors for some time, appearing successfully as a pinch-hitter for the 1950 Giants.

Leave it to voluble Dizzy Dean to get himself mixed up in a scandal of sorts. The season was 1937 and for Diz it was probably his most eventful one—most eventful Diz Dean season for all baseball, in fact. That Diz got off on the wrong foot in '37 is readily seen in his spring training action of slugging sportswriter Jack Miley in a Tampa, Florida hotel. The season was but briefly under way when Diz again knotted his fists and "swang" a couple of haymakers at his own first-baseman, Rip Collins, because the pair had the misfortune to collide head-on fielding a grounder. Then when Umpire George Barr called a balk on Dizzy during another Card contest, Dean turned right around and called both the umpire and National League president Ford Frick "a couple of crooks."

Followed by a sizzling suspension by Mr. Frick until Diz agreed to call off the conflict by means of a written apology, Dean, stubborn as a Missouri mule, balked, for sure this time. Only the accomplished hand of Ford Frick prevented Dean's disaster. The league leader said nothing and then one day quietly un-suspended Diz, as Dean himself would say it.

In the clear again, Dizzy Dean proceeded to work his way right back into the league doghouse by deciding to take a holiday rather than lend his valuable arm to the All-Star game in Washington. This time it took Sam Breadon's smooth salve to rub Dizzy the right way and thanks to the Cardinal boss, Dizzy Dean didn't become baseball's number one outcast. Yet, Ole Diz may have had a feeling in his bones about that All-Star game for it was in this contest of 1937 that he injured the big toe which put an end to his prolific pitching period.

In June, 1949 the Phillies were in Chicago for a series with the Chicago Cubs. Nobody figured it to be a particularly eventful series but it made more headlines than a September stretch pennant dog fight. It was on this Philly-Cub occasion that the shot was fired which echoed around the baseball world. Philly first sacker Eddie Waitkus was shot by a deranged bobbysoxer and critically wounded.

Had not Eddie been a genuinely straight guy of exemplary behavior, here could have been a super scandal in the making with the handsome ball player responding to a note summoning him to the Chicago hotel room of Ann Ruth Steinhagen. "I have something very important to tell you," said the note in effect. "Come to my room at once."

Unsuspecting and curious, the Philly fellow walked into the den of the lioness. As he entered, Eddie stared into the muzzle of a revolver and fell badly wounded when a slug tore through him. At length the deranged girl was placed in a mental institution and Eddie Waitkus—well, he made the greatest comeback in the history of baseball, leading the Phillies to their first pennant in 35 years during 1950 with his classy first-sacking and his leadoff punch.

The year 1920 saw the last five-out-of-nine World Series, won by the Indians five games to Brooklyn's two. Oddly enough, the Dodgers captured two straight at Brooklyn after dropping the first encounter and then they were blitzed in four straight tilts in the Indian wigwam. What threw a damper on Flatbush spirits was the queer behavior of ace Brooklyn hurler, the famous Rube Marquard.

Cops pinched the scintillating southpaw at his Cleveland hotel room on a charge of scalping tickets. Law officers declared Rube was attempting to peddle eight box seats for $400. Rube probably didn't realize the seriousness of his actions and the incident coming on top of the 1919 Black Sox episode created a fantastic fuss in the papers. Poor Rube was set free but didn't get the chance to further Brooklyn's cause any more in the disastrous Series.

Brooklyn club president, Harry Ebbets, went on a rampage and firmly announced Marquard would never again wear a Dodger uniform. The pitcher's Series salary was held back until he was sentenced by a Cleveland judge: fine, one dollar plus costs. Next season the Rube did all his chucking for the Cincinnati Reds.

It was inevitable that a precocious personality like Babe Ruth should get mixed up in what could have developed into a couple of baseball's juiciest scandals of sorts. Anybody around at the time, 1922, knew that when headstrong Babe ran up against equally adamant Judge Kenesaw Mountain Landis, baseball's new commissioner, explosions were bound to occur. And they did.

The good judge had slapped a stern directive against post-season barnstorming of any kind, but Babe Ruth and Bob Meusel winked at the Kenesaw communique and hit the hinterlands to gather up a few fast bucks. "You get forty days of suspension for that escapade," decreed the judicial veteran. "Oh yeh," snapped the Bambino in no uncertain terms.

Considerably miffed, the Judge nonetheless kept a firm two lips and said nothing; even he knew the Babe was Mr. Baseball. The fracas flattened itself out nice and neatly and all was well with the diamond doings of Sir Ruth in 1922, at least for a while.

Before long Babe Ruth was back in striped Yankee uniform, only to throw dirt in ungentlemanly fashion into the face of an umpire and he added thunder to the madcap adventure by jumping into the stands and chasing a heckling fan clear out of the ball park. Anybody but the immortal Babe could have drawn a lengthy suspension or worse for such tactless tactics. At any rate, it is fortunate for baseball (and for the fan) that the Babe never could quite catch up with him.

Luckily for the big Babe, American League president Ban Johnson handled the double deportment deficiency of the Babe's and Ban was extremely lenient with the Bam. "Be a good boy," cajoled Johnson, fining the garrulous guy a pithy $200 and stripping him of his rank as Yankee field captain.

Still, the Babe wasn't to be field-broken. During the World Series he and Meusel invaded the privacy of the Giant's clubhouse to trounce George Rawlings for making uncomplimentary remarks on the field of play and only the wise intervention of other ball players and some newspaper reporters prevented Babe Ruth from getting into an even bigger mess.

Eight members of the Chicago White Sox were banished from baseball for the "fix" of the 1919 World Series. Just one season earlier, in 1918, Cincinnati first-baseman Hal Chase had made a forced appearance before league moguls on charges of propositioning other Rhineland players with cash efforts to throw ball games. On top of this, manager Christy Mathewson had berated Hal for deliberately making bad throws to pitchers covering first base on grounders down his way. Because Chase's Cincinnati teammates refused to testify, nothing came of the affair except the rapid transfer of Hal Chase to New York. Luckily Hal didn't make that infamous 1919 Series.

It appears Judge Landis happened upon the league scene in time, perhaps to save the game from deteriorating into the farce of wrestling. Giant southpaw Phil Douglas is on record as having contacted Les Mann of the Cards with a most unusual offer. The Giant chucker informed Mann that he, Douglas, could be persuaded not to pitch in a crucial Giant-Card series if the Redbirds would make it worth his while. Mann handed the Douglas missive over to Branch Rickey who in turn flipped the hot potato to Judge

Landis. The fiery commissioner flamed. Summoning Douglas to his chamber of terrors, Landis promptly secured a confession and gave the New York moundsman the bounce from baseball.

The poor Giants of that era unfortunately came up with more than their share of questionable characters. No more than two years later, Cozy Dolan and Jimmy O'Connell hatched up a plot to buy off Philly shortstop Heinie Sand for $500 thereby practically sewing up a pennant for the New Yorkers. An honest guy, Sand went straight to his manager, Art Fletcher, who lost no time in getting the bombshell into the lap of league prexy John Heydler. Then Judge Landis heard and snapped to action, confronting the conspirators on the spot along with other players who had heard of the abortive offer. O'Connell and Dolan packed up and left baseball with lifetime suspensions in their baggage.

The word "scandal" was hurled around National League quarters during the season of 1912. At that time Horace Fogel was president of the Philadelphia Phillies, although in actuality he was really nothing more than a front for Charley Murphy, Cub owner, who controlled both teams. Such an arrangement today would be considered intolerable; in fact Branch Rickey of the Dodgers in 1950 had to go slow while seeking to unload his Brooklyn holdings and trying to land a job elsewhere at the same time.

Fogel was a stormy individual who accused umpires of deliberately calling decisions against his team. On top of this, Horace tried to cast a stigma on the entire league by accusing rival managers of playing weak or strong lineups on different days depending upon the opposition.

That Fogel had to be silenced was the byword around National League front offices, so the association held a private trial for Fogel at the close of the 1912 season. Found guilty, Fogel was forced to withdraw forever from baseball. Yet, as in all cases of the kind, the odor lingered.

Although football and boxing annually produce more than their share of deaths in action, modern major league's lone fatality almost provoked a solid scandal. The mortally wounded victim was Cleveland shortstop Ray Chapman, beaned by a fast ball in the Polo Grounds where the Indians were facing the Yanks. Pitcher on the sorrowful afternoon was submarine-ball swiftie Carl Mays. What made the outlook black for Mays were charges of "bean-ball" and of deliberately hitting Chapman. Four American League clubs even threatened to strike against the truculent thrower.

The affair at length died down, largely due to the behavior of Mays. An acknowledged hard-hitting, trigger-tempered competitor, Carl Mays showed genuine and tremendous concern over the tragedy. His own behavior was more than enough to vindicate Mays.

In case you've ever wondered about the major-league rule prohibiting player swaps after the June 15 deadline—except for waiver sales—it came about in 1922 thanks to a vigorous protest by Branch Rickey which almost precipitated a scandal of proportions. The National League race that season had been a wing-dinger until August, the month the Giants just about sewed up the flag by shamelessly purchasing outstanding hurler Hugh McQuillan from the Braves for $100,000 and another pitcher named Joe. The action put the Boston team in a far from favorable position as McQuillan was exactly the medicine needed by the Giants for a cinch flag.

Added strength was lent to the Rickey crusade later in the very same season when the Yankees purchased sorely needed third-baseman Joe Dugan from the Boston Red Sox. The addition of the dependable Dugan gave the Yanks that certain something extra which enabled them to shade the St. Louis Browns for the league title by a scant game.

The furor reached a fever pitch with accusations of collusion and favoritism tossed off in a rising crescendo. Judge Landis could no longer close his ears to the din. He issued a proclamation which still stands: "Except for waivers, no more player deals after June 15." For emphasis he gave a violent nod of his white head.

Behind Closed Doors

Much of the drama of baseball is acted out behind closed doors, in the offices of the club presidents and general managers or in the chambers of the league presidents. Many of baseball's most interesting news stories are born off the playing field. Even gatherings of ordinary baseball fans frequently break out in front-office or league-headquarters talk, rather than in debate about the respective merits of individual ball players.

Happy Chandler who donned the well-worn robe of baseball Czar Judge Kenesaw Mountain Landis when the latter passed from the national scene has been the subject of much newsprint controversy. A former United States Senator from Kentucky, Happy has not had a happy time of it in general from the pens of America's sports scribes. Then late in 1950 came the startling withdrawal of support by club owners for Commissioner Chandler, who had previously been solidly entrenched, and news of his struggle to hold onto his job and his determination not to give up without a fight in spite of tremendous odds, which of course in the end he had to give up.

Although Judge Landis is looked on by most outside observers as the saint of baseball, his popularity among club owners was open to debate. For one thing, most owners resented the Judge's unlimited power, feeling no man should assume such importance. Likewise, the choice of Happy Chandler was not universal; friend Larry MacPhail was most responsible for riding the Kentucky gentleman through as baseball commissioner although at the time there were more than a few dissenters.

In the case of Judge Landis, his iron-clad authority was really challenged on only one occasion, away back in 1931 and by Phil Ball, owner of the Browns at the time. Ball resented the action of Landis in declaring a St. Louis farmhand, outfielder Fred Bennett, a free agent. So Mr. Ball resorted to the courts of law in Milwaukee.

"The major-league agreement recognizes the office of the Commissioner and the jurisdiction aforesaid and provides that in case of any dispute between any major club and any minor club the disputants may certify the dispute to the Commissioner for decision and that the determination shall be final."

That's the way Federal Court Judge Walter Lindley ruled, adding that the various agreements and rules, constituting a complete code for, or charter and bylaws of, organized baseball in America disclose a clear intent upon the part of the parties to endow the Commissioner with all the attributes of a benevolent but absolute despot and all the disciplinary powers of the proverbial pater familias.

Naturally owner Ball was quite unhappy about the results. He did go so far as to threaten an appeal but when Landis threatened to resign, Ball decided to drop the entire matter.

In later years, Leslie O'Connor, general manager of the White Sox, threatened similar action in a row over a high school player with Happy Chandler. In this case, however, O'Connor listened to the advice of fellow baseball executives and stayed away from the courts of law for several reasons. Baseball's risky reserve clause contract was under criticism in the press and Chandler's complete authority would be questioned severely in any event, something no major-league mogul wanted to have happen.

Curious are the circumstances, sometimes, under which a ball club may change ownership virtually overnight. This sort of thing happened in 1950 to Frank McKinney, president of the Pittsburgh Pirates at the time. Complaining of ill health, McKinney accepted the suggestion of his physician to check in at the hospital for a cardiogram. He was immediately ordered to bed.

The tone was ominous and Frank feared for his life. As a result he lost little time in selling out his interest in the Pirates to John Galbreath. Two or three days later Frank McKinney learned the awful truth. The electricity in the hospital had been found faulty and the only thing wrong with his heart was it had been in his throat after the incorrect cardiogram!

Cactus grew too slowly for Bill Veeck's taste. That's why big Bill returned to baseball in 1946 as president of the Cleveland Indians after a fling as an Arizona rancher. The phrase is bombastic Bill's own and describes the beehive known as Bill Veeck better than any other words.

That Bill Veeck was a sure shot in the arm for baseball, Cleveland Indian fashion, is proved by a glance at the figures. Before Bill took over the helm of the Indians, Cleveland had never drawn more than a million fans in one season. With Bill as boss man from

1946 to 1949 the Indians twice topped the million mark and twice went over the two-million top, which is par for any course, of course. The Cleveland outfit is unique, by the way, in that it does not play on its own field but in a municipally operated stadium.

Bill's success is built considerably on his flare for promotion, and of course the ranking teams he gave the Cleveland fans are not to be passed over lightly. A young, aggressive fellow still in his early thirties when he put the Indians in a sound financial tepee, Veeck inherited his talents naturally from a father who was once president of the Chicago Cubs.

To Bill Veeck's credit go a lot of laurels. He was the first to spur ticket sales by establishing a telephone switchboard, giving the fans opportunity to talk personally with Cleveland club officials. Much of Vitamin Veeck's time was spent on the rubber-chicken circuit, as an after-dinner speaker on the virtues of the Cleveland nine.

Next move on the part of Veeck the promoter was to broadcast his games—something the previous owners had shunned like radioactive atoms—and to clean up the ball park which also meant instilling the spirit of friendliness in ushers and other park personnel. As a matter of fact, keen as Veeck was for radio, he is just as enthusiastic for television. "It's good promotion," is the Bill Veeck way of describing the video camera condemned by many owners for sagging attendances.

Veeck's promotion extended all the way to the charities, as he honestly felt the city's major-league ball club should do something for the people who were indirectly doing something for the team. The Cleveland Indians gave to the Community Fund and the Cleveland Indians arranged for a series of exhibition games with the Brooklyn Dodgers to aid amateur baseball.

In short, the success of blond, husky Bill Veeck, the man with the open collar, in organized baseball's front office seems built upon a charitable attitude toward the fan, an avenue travelled perhaps by too few major-league magnates.

Clark Griffith was probably more successful with the Washington Senators when he was managing them than when he was owning them. Aside from a few unusual seasons, Griffith's Washington entry has occupied the second division of the American League with some consistency. However, the year he took over as manager of the Nats, 1912, he elevated the shabby franchise to second place and he came right back next season to duplicate the feat.

Griffith could be classed as one of the last Trader Horns of baseball. True, he sold a few of his stars for stupendous sums; yet he always has been willing to swap players or to engage in larger transactions involving blocks of baseballers. A curious aspect of the Clark Griffith swap system is his willingness to bring back players he has traded away seasons before.

Most notable of Griff's "bring 'em back while they're alive" system concerns Bucky Harris who has been hired to manage the Washington Senators on three different occasions, no less! Cast off as skipper in 1928, Harris was hired back in 1934. Then in 1950 Griffith signed up Bucky Harris as field boss of the Senators for the third time.

In 1946 Griffith traded speedy outfielder George Case to Cleveland for socking outfielder Jeff Heath. Apparently the Old Fox regretted the deal for one short year later he sent star pitcher Roger Wolff to the Indians for the very same George Case. First-baseman Zeke Bonura and Joe Kuhel are two outstanding examples of the send-them-away, bring-them-back Clark Griffith project.

Back in 1927 Griffith traded star infielder Buddy Myer to the Red Sox for a shortstop who lasted less than a season with the club. Apparently Clark regretted that move so much he opened the sacks wide to get Buddy back in Washington livery. Exactly two years later, the Washington prexy handed over five valuable players to the Red Sox for the self-same Buddy Myer who justified the faith of his former boss by going on to big things in the Capitol city.

One of the wonders of baseball was Wilbert Robinson who usually managed the Brooklyn Dodgers and sometimes acted as president during his 18 year tenure with the Daffy Dans. Better known as Uncle Robbie, Robinson assumed management of the Brooks in 1914.

Never allowing himself a bundle of cash with which to work deals—even when he was club president—the round, old Baltimore Oriole star catcher was in a class by himself in reclaiming fallen athletes, particularly pitchers. Among the errant moundsmen righted by Robbie were stellar slabsters like Jack Coombs, Burleigh Grimes, Larry Cheney and Rube Marquard, to mention a few. It was Robbie who boosted Grimes to stardom after burly Burleigh had washed out in Pittsburgh. With Brooklyn the hard-boiled spitballer was a constant winner. Uncle Robbie helped Dazzy Vance, the lazy and hard-throwing righthander, to become one of baseball's immortals after other major league clubs had passed off the Dazzler as not good enough.

Another of Robinson's discoveries was of course Babe Herman, one of baseball's better hitters and all-time screwballs. When they were both teammates, pitcher Dazzy Vance tried to describe Herman's hitting ability and got off his classic comment: "Babe is a hard guy to outthink, because how can you outthink a guy who doesn't think?" In 1931 both Babe Herman and Wilbert Robinson left the Dodgers and there passed an era unique in the annals of baseball.

Del Webb, who bought into the New York Yankees at the height of the Larry MacPhail regime, is a genuine, honest-to-goodness Horatio Alger story. Son of a not too prosperous carpenter, Del tried to earn a living from his real love, baseball, and became a pretty fair side-armed righthander until his wing went dead. Not much choice remained for Del but to switch back to the hammer and saw and build himself a foundation.

And what a foundation Del Webb constructed. Without a surplus of education, hard-working Webb used his carpentry tools to build a million-dollar empire. The so-so righthander who failed dismally at baseball came along financially to buy his way into the richest club in baseball.

That's not all. Del Webb became a partner in Bing Crosby Enterprises, the croon king's far-flung organization covering a multitude of commercial setups. All in all, Del Webb heads probably more than a score of assorted corporations himself. He has built everything from army barracks to classy hotels. Del Webb once owned the Kansas City Blues of the old American Association, and entrepreneur that he is, he is also big in real estate in the West.

Pooling a cool $2,800,000, Del Webb, Dan Topping and Larry MacPhail picked up the Yankees with its lucrative farm system from the heirs of Jacob Ruppert. To be sure, this was a sound baseball bargain engineered by a triumvirate of shrewd business operators.

The new régime became a rocky one fired by the uncontrollable temper of Col. Larry MacPhail. After the 1947 World Series, won by the Yanks from Brooklyn, four games to three, MacPhail blew his top and created havoc in baseball's gentlemanly circles by firing his able vice-president, George Weiss, and by socking Brooklyn secretary, John McDonald. Then Larry got into a ripping row with his partner, Dan Topping. It was with an honest sigh of relief that Del Webb and Dan Topping put a million in cash on the line to induce loud Larry's resignation. The pair's first move on their own was to hire back the canny farm system director, George Weiss, this time as general manager.

Since his high school days George Weiss has been one of the brains behind the baseball scenes. At Hillhouse High School, New Haven, Weiss wasn't able enough to make the team but he did become its manager. His solid education included study at Yale from where he went on to managing semi-pro ball teams.

Then came the New Haven team of the Eastern League back in 1919 for George Weiss. Ten years at New Haven and George took another step up the ladder, on to Baltimore in the International League. Col. Jake Ruppert didn't have to look far for the man he wanted to run his expanding farm system. He chose George Weiss and affable Georgie did a bangup job for all of 16 seasons. A tribute to the ivory hunting ability of George Weiss is the fact that seven of the nine pennant-winning Yankees of 1947 were brought up from New York farm clubs.

To his dying day George Weiss will never be able to understand how the fantastic finger of lady luck pointed in the opposite direction when death brushed against his elbow. It happened back in 1923 as young Weiss was en route to attend the season's minor-league meetings. Weiss and Wild Bill Donovan, his manager at New Haven and former big-league pitching star, were having a debate as to who should sleep in the upper berth during the train trip, so George pulled his rank and won the upper.

Tragedy rode the rails that night as the train crashed, killing Donovan and eight others, all occupying lowers. As for George Weiss, he was blasted clear through the roof of the wrecked car and was looked upon as a goner. Weiss surprised medical men by leaving the hospital little more than a month later and resuming his minor-league executive duties.

The death of Judge Kenesaw Mountain Landis after a long and admittedly successful stint as Czar of baseball saw the rise of another man to the position, a man of a different nature and possibly of less tact than the outspoken Landis. This man was Albert B. (Happy) Chandler. Yet, but for the obstinacy of the late President Franklin D. Roosevelt, Happy Chandler might have become President of the United States, not just president of all organized baseball.

The onetime Governor of Kentucky and Senator from the same state had the backing of many Democrats to run as Vice-President on the Roosevelt ticket in 1944. The arrangement came close to actuality, except for one important catch. Roosevelt insisted upon—and got—Senator Harry S. Truman as his lieutenant. It is doubtful though whether Happy Chandler could have drawn more criticism as President of the United States than as president of organized baseball.

For a good many years the front offices of the St. Louis Browns and the St. Louis Cardinals have been at it with little love being lost between either club. As far back as 1927 the Browns tried to kick the Cards out of the former's ball park, Sportsman's Park. As the Red Birds held a 14-year lease, the Brownies were naturally unsuccessful.

Undaunted, the American League landlords tried similar action again early in 1949. With the starting date for the season only a few weeks off, the Browns dropped a bombshell by demanding the Cardinals go find themselves a new home by an April 1 deadline. To be sure, the Cards were stunned. Where could they play? Still, they had no cause for worry since after all, they did possess that lease.

What rankled the Browns most was the rent paid them by the Cardinals, a pithy $35,000 in those years of soaring prices. What's more, the Browns have been a losing proposition consistently and they honestly need the extra cash. What the future brings should be interesting for with the defense effort accelerated, it is doubtful the Cardinals will get permission to build their own ball yard for some years to come.

Perhaps you have pondered over the problem of how much interest in general has been shown baseball by Presidents of the United States. Well, away back in 1915, Woodrow Wilson became the first President on record to attend a World Series game and he helped launch things handsomely in the second game by throwing out the ball to get activities under way.

As a major-league baseball player Hank Greenberg was always a standout, not only at the dish whacking out home runs but as an all-around gentleman and sportsman. In close to 15 seasons with the Tigers of Detroit, Hammering Hank blasted better than 300 home runs, usually knocked in at least 100 runs per season and hit in the neighborhood of .300 quite consistently. Naturally it came as quite a shock to Hank when Detroit dispensed with his services at the close of the 1946 season.

It would be folly to declare Hank needed the dough. As a ten-year-plus star Hank earned more than his share of greenbacks for Greenberg. Then too, in 1946 the Bronx bomber married attractive Carol Gimbel, and you don't need Macy's to tell you Gimbel's Department Store does more than eke out a scanty living. A low bow goes to Hank for his genuine interest in baseball when you consider he could have retired from the national pastime to more lucrative, less risky pastures.

After a lone slugging season with the Pittsburgh Pirates Hank called quits to a brilliant active career. It was with considerable enthusiasm that followers of the sport saw Hank come back a year or so later in an executive capacity with the Cleveland Indians, vice-president and director of the farm system. Some sceptics smirked and called it a publicity deal, but the guy from the Bronx soon changed their minds.

"Never have I seen any one with more ability, more drive, more common sense than Hank Greenberg." Those are the quoted words of Eddie Stumpf, business manager of the Cleveland farm system.

Greenberg had to do a heap of learning to grasp the importance of his front-office position, but in no time at all he was master of the job. The same thing held true for big Greenberg many years earlier when he had been a gawky kid with plenty of raw power but little skill or finesse. Hank came to baseball a .200 hitter with a reputation for blasting the long one when he got his pitch. Well known is the story about how Hank showed up at the Detroit ball park every morning to practice for hours strictly on his own. In no time at all, Hank upped his puny percentage and became known as a guy who could no longer "be pitched to."

For Hank to carry out the same thoroughness in a front-office capacity is only natural. Addressing springtime rookies, Hank the baseball businessman, always tells them that success in baseball is just like at any other job, plenty of hard work. "Those who don't want to work hard might as well give it up while there is still time to turn to something else."

Those who have operated with him compliment

Hank on his scrupulous honesty. If a rookie doesn't have it, Hank tells him, sparing the kid delusions of a grandeur never to be achieved. For his tryout sessions Hank climbed into baseball uniform just like everybody else. Regular hours were observed and there was no hit-and-miss attitude about the entire procedure.

Acquaintances insist Hank Greenberg is destined to rank with the all-time greats of the baseball business world just as he rated as a headline maker on the baseball field.

Although Branch Rickey grabbed the spotlight, there are many who insist the late Sam Breadon was the real shining light behind the success of the St. Louis Cardinals. If Sam Breadon sparkled in one respect, it was in his undaunted and undying community spirit. He loved the city of St. Louis. Furthermore, you can't overlook the accomplishments of Sam the man. In 24 St. Louis baseball seasons Breadon brought home nine pennants and six world championships, better than par for any baseball course.

Sam was the first man to put on a Sunday doubleheader in St. Louis, a move copied by every other club in both circuits. In Brooklyn, Sam's man, Branch Rickey, eliminated the Sunday double-header and this move did baseball no good at all. In earlier days Sam and Branch of course did get together to put the widely duplicated farm system on a firm footing.

Though Sam Breadon was considered ruthless in disposing of favorite players who had passed their primes, he was kind in dealing with faded favorites who found themselves in financial distress. This side of Sam was not generally known—Sam the softie, Sam the easy touch.

On a business level Sam was different. Explaining his frequent sales of stars, Sam would declare, "I won't have dead wood on my club. I need new blood to keep up the power of my teams."

Newspapermen soon learned that Sam was a man of his word. He never contradicted a previous statement and he never said anything he did not honestly mean at the time. Without a doubt Sam Breadon brought more stars to baseball than any single individual before or after.

Frank C. Lane, general manager of the Chicago White Sox, figured he could add power to his lineup by investing a few fast bucks in a parcel of chicken wire. It was Lane's brainstorm to increase the home-run power of his 1949 White Sox by stringing the chicken wire in front of the outfield thereby shortening the distance for the long ball by a weak hitter.

The $5,000 investment for the chicken wire was chicken feed and succeeded in lessening the distance by some 20 feet to all parts of the stands. With the home run in vogue in modern-day baseball, leader Lane drew no opposition from other clubs and it was his shrewd observation that the move would put a couple of White Sox sluggers right up there in the four-play derby.

How Frank Lane's brainstorm exploded can best be explained by the statistics which showed other clubs outhomering the White Sox almost 2 to 1 with the weaker clubs of the league joining the merrymaking against the Pale Hose. Club followers traced at least three important home team losses to the chicken coop.

The season was only a few weeks old when Frank C. Lane removed the chicken wire from Comiskey Park. With only three teams—Washington, Detroit and St. Louis—having had potshots at the shortie, Lane shuddered when he thought of what the hard-hitting Yanks and Red Sox would do to his short wall. In short, Lane's chicken-wire trap set for the enemy was only serving as barbed wire against his own team.

Leagues, Leagues, Leagues!

As might be expected, big-league baseball has not been without its competition throughout the years, the American League, set up in opposition to the older National, serving as a good example. A tribute to the men who have guided big-league baseball successfully was the 75th anniversary celebration of the National League in 1951. The big damper on the observance was the fierce fighting by American soldiers in Korea.

The National League took over in 1876 from its predecessor, The National Association, which about that time was enjoying its final gasps. Plans for the then new loop were advanced largely by a Chicago businessman and sportsman, William A. Hulbert. Founding purposes of the National League were to (1) encourage, foster and elevate the game of baseball, (2) enact and enforce proper rules and (3) make the game respectable and honorable.

If baseball were practiced today as it was in the old days the game would command little respect. Players were paid little and consequently they made frequent deals with gamblers to pull a betting coup, thereby adding a bit to their low incomes. Exactly 13 clubs made up the National League's forerunner, the National Association, and it was at best a hodgepodge sort of affair with clubs raiding one another's personnel in an effort to get better talent.

William A. Hulbert himself was guilty of similar conduct. Exactly one season before he helped found the National League, Hulbert, as president of the Chicago team, made a deal with four Boston players to move over to his Chicago entry on the following season. Refusing to take such high-handed action sitting down, Boston President N. T. Apolonio tried to outlaw from disorganized baseball both crusader Hulbert and A. G. Spalding, the game's number-one pitcher who was one of the quartet to jump Boston for Chicago. That's what gave Hulbert the idea of starting another league, nothing more noble.

Hulbert was able to swing his new league with a little behind-the-scenes manipulation and a number of clubs from the old Association reluctantly joined the newcomer loop. First president of the National League was Morgan B. Bulkeley of the Hartford entry, a man who later advanced to Governor of Connecticut and U. S. Senator.

"The National League of Professional Baseball Clubs," was the official title of the new league. Most of the Association clubs remained in the setup with only Cincinnati and Louisville added. Harmony, however, was not to be achieved. The weak sister clubs of the league—New York and Philadelphia—refused to go on a western trip and so were kicked out of competition entirely. As a result, at the end of the first season the league presidency changed hands with Bulkeley going out and William Hulbert taking over. Poor Hulbert had to struggle through several juicy gambling stenches with but a six-team league.

Things went from bad to worse financially, and

the 1878 season saw baseball almost come to an un-
timely death as only three cities could afford to field
teams in the National League which had lost five
franchises in only a couple of years. Somehow, President Hulbert scraped together sufficient second-class
cities to make it an official season but in 1879 he ran
into trouble again. This time he added four new cities
to bring the National League miraculously to full
strength of eight.

When Hulbert and league directors gave the heave-
ho to Cincinnati after the end of the 1880 season, only
Chicago and Boston remained of the original eight-
some! Evidently the National League was too much
even for a spirited leader like Hulbert for the loop
prexy died of a heart attack in 1882, his place taken
by A. G. Mills, a New York attorney.

No less than five times has the power of the National
League been challenged, with the only successful in-
surrection producing the American league officially
recognized in 1900. Independent teams also rose up
to contest the authority of the new league and some
thrived, notably in Philadelphia, Brooklyn and Washington.

The American Association was born in 1882 and
since it incorporated several of the more popular independent clubs, the loop promptly put itself on an
equal level of ability with the National League. On
top of this, the American Association played baseball
at cut-rate prices. Quickly, new National League
president, Colonel Mills, established peace between
the two leagues.

Along about 1884 a Union League popped into the

picture to throw baseball topsy-turvy again what with all the wrinkles having been straightened out by means of the previous peace pledge between the Nationals and Americans a few seasons before. Critics of today's baseball player contract will be interested to know that the Union League came about chiefly to combat baseball's reserve clause which was a source of keen controversy away back in those days.

Naturally, the new Union League raided the rosters of established American and National franchises to recruit name ball players. Some disgruntled performers switched to the third big league but soon regretted it when the latest loop experienced tremendous financial difficulties and switched teams from one city to another almost overnight to make things go. Later, the rebel players were admitted back to their original teams in the National and American leagues upon payment of a modest fine.

Repercussions of the player-conduct in bolting the established leagues for the bootleg Union League brought about the resignation of league prexy Mills. He was succeeded by Nicholas E. Young, who as Uncle Nick served in that capacity for 16 long seasons. And with the Union League folded and tucked away after a disastrous single season, organized baseball enjoyed comparative peace for about five years.

Then along came baseball's biggest labor dispute which blossomed into a baseball schism and formation of another independent circuit, the Players League. About this time ball players had organized into a National Brotherhood of Baseball Players which centered attacks on the still-controversial reserve clause which kept a player in the employ of his parent club often against his better wishes and best judgment.

The Players League was a novelty in that, though backed by outside funds, each of the eight clubs in key cities was headed by a popular ball player of the day. Furthermore, the actual ball players in the league drew bigger salaries than they had in the National League and all athletes were marked down to share in the profits of the club.

The National League attempted to bolster its position by bringing in stronger franchises from the fading American Association. Yet, more than half of the league's top players deserted to what they called their own loop, the Players League. A good proportion of American Association standouts joined their National League brethren in galloping off to the confines of the new circuit. Some clubs actually lost their entire teams intact to the outlaw league!

In the 1890 baseball war years major league baseball clubs were actually weakened more than they were in the later World War years of 1941-45 when almost every team was relieved of its stars. In point of fact, the Players League presented a more capable collection of ball players than did the senior circuits.

The National League brought the battle right into the backyard of the Players League which seemed bent on pursuing more peaceful paths. Games were scheduled to conflict with encounters among Players teams at almost every opportunity. Naturally, the results were ruinous.

Attendance figures were padded on both sides to

point out that "our league is the BIG league." Every trick was tried by both sides including checks on actual attendance figures by spies. Feeling ran high and it is remarkable no bad blood was spilled. Observers of the day claimed the Players League appeared to attract more attention but by no means enjoyed a successful season.

At the end of 1890, the Players League was not able to carry on. Leaders sold their franchises back to the National League. The war was over, but not for long. As for the National League, it willingly accepted back all rebellious players and did not even so much as breathe a threat of punitive action.

One war ended and another began as the American Association became miffed over player raids by its rival National League and withdrew from the peace agreement drawn up some years before. Although no additional shanghaiing of players occurred and no serious disturbances came about, the two leagues vied with each other for public power.

Came another upheaval at the close of the 1891 season when the American Association and National League merged into a League-Association, embracing all of 12 clubs.

In much the manner of the Pacific Coast League in more modern times, the old Western League of the turn of the century sought elevation to major-league status. However, the Westerners of olden times would not take no for an answer and when they were denied permission to improve their station in life, they went into competition with the National League by calling themselves the American League

and establishing themselves in several defunct cities of the older loop. Commanding General of the American League uprising was youthful Ban Johnson.

What made the American League's position more difficult was a threatened revival of the old American Association which would produce a topheavy total of three big leagues. Realizing that action was essential, American League leaders paid National League stars more handsome salaries to skip to the new loop. Many did.

Again price-cutting figured in the operation with the American League putting bunches of seats on the line at 25 cents each. Prexy Johnson also went all out to get ladies to attend the ball parks. Then in 1901, the American League really went into high gear.

Competition among both leagues for outstanding player personnel became tremendous and some players gleefully hopped back and forth between both loops, bettering their salary checks with each move. To top it all off, the National League was having a blazing intra-camp warfare and could not agree upon a league president. Naturally, the American League rubbed happy hands over the National League strife.

Pittsburgh was the only National League club not dealt a deadly blow by the player-snatching junior loop, so the Pirates walked away from the rest of the field in 1902 competition, winning the pennant by an unbelievable 27½ games over the second-place Brooklyn entry. At this point John McGraw switched back to the National League from the American League to become a lifelong enemy of senior loop leader, Ban Johnson. They never spoke to each other again.

Overcoming many minor difficulties, the American League continued to make a go of it and after two seasons of successful play managed to persuade additional National Leaguers to desert the old for the new. To bolster its fading strength, the National League sought more forceful leadership and signed enterprising Harry Pulliam to the league presidency in 1902.

Before the 1903 season saw light, the National League made peace overtures and tried to absorb the rebels into its own loop. This failing, desperate National League club owners agreed to a peace pact and recognition in full of the senior circuit. Certain considerations were agreed upon and both leagues prospered in almost complete harmony for about 15 tame years with perhaps one or two minor disturbances.

The year 1914 saw war break out on both the battle-fields of Europe and on the baseball playing fields of America. Again another league tried to break the domination of the elders, this time claiming to be a third big league and calling itself the Federal League. The financially solvent Federal managed to survive two lean seasons.

Actually, the Federal League was more or less an outgrowth of its predecessor called the United States League in 1912 and finally the Federal League in 1913, but lacking name stars, it didn't cause much of a stir. Then along came some money and the Federal League was right in the thick of the time-worn attendance fight. In Brooklyn, for example, the Ward Baking Company backed a league entry.

Because organized baseball owners agreed to boost the salaries of their stars, the older loops did not lose players in wholesale lots. Yet, some diamond dandies did desert to the Federal League, fellows like Bill McKechnie who became a Hall of Famer. Hal Chase was another of the better-known jumpers.

Following the precedent set by the American League back before the turn of the century, the Feds used the same tactics to fight the same organization, the Americans—as well as the Nationals—by setting up teams in many cities occupied by clubs of either or both older leagues. This time the Federal League took up the cudgels against the operations of organized baseball by claiming the older leagues were violating the Sherman Antitrust Act. Their appeal went to Judge Landis who was later to become protector of baseball's controversial rules as Czar of the majors. Judge Landis handled the situation in peculiar fashion by never handing down a decision — his hand left unforced by the dissolution of the Federal League after the close of the 1915 season.

The Federal-organized baseball war made things rough all around, the minor leagues feeling the sting of excess competition as well. Clubs went from one city to another, seeking a home site free from cut-throat operations. Some estimates placed the two-year battle at a cost of ten million dollars.

The death of the Federal League was blamed in part on the international situation. War clouds, stirred up in Europe, were drifting toward the United States. What happened was a sort of armistice on the part of the Federal League. They were equipped apparently to carry on the warfare but they succumbed to a pay-off, on the part of both the National and American Leagues, to suspend operations.

A number of Federal League commanders were permitted to buy into organized baseball clubs. Some took their players with them; other athletes were put into a common pool for a draft with National and American League teams buying back many of their former performers from the Feds. As in previous revolutions, none of the ball players who jumped the majors was denied re-entry.

Following 1915 came the golden age of baseball and except for a business depression which hit every commercial enterprise in this country, the major and minor leagues rolled their merry ways without the slightest threat of unauthorized competition. The sublime condition existed until one Jorge Pasquel, wealthy Mexican, waved dollars under the noses of established American big-leaguers in a move to bring them south of the border, thereby bolstering his Mexican League.

Although the foundation of Mexican baseball in opposition to the giant USA industry seemed false, Jorge's money didn't, and many dissatisfied Yankee toilers looked with interest on the Pasquel paycheck. Some accepted and many won salary battles with their owners by threatening to jump. Such stars as Vern Stephens, star Brown shortstop, and Phil Rizzuto, equally talented New York Yankee shortfielder, actually packed bags with Stephens making his way south over the Rio Grande only to change his mind and return.

Hardest hit club in the majors as a result of the Pasquel raids was St. Louis, never famous for exactly overpaying its athletes. The Cards lost two ace pitchers, Max Lanier and Fred Martin, as well as valuable infielder Lou Klein. Actually gorgeous Jorge was after bigger game, making offers to standouts like Stan Musial and Enos Slaughter but without success. Brooklyn, which battled St. Louis to a National League tie in the 1946 standings only to lose the play-off, also suffered at the hands of Pasquel, surrendering star catcher Mickey Owen and slugging outfielder Louis Olmo to the Latin league forces. Promptly, Commissioner Happy Chandler slapped a five-year ban on all players who had treated the majors with such contempt.

Sal Maglie was scarcely looked upon as one of the biggest operators to leave organized baseball for the Mexican loop. Even the Giants who needed pitching like a flower needs water brushed lightly the departure of solid Sal. The Giants figured they had plenty of pitchers like Sal; what they wanted were a couple standouts like Raschi, Sain or Newhouser.

How wrong the Giants were in their estimation of him was proved by Sal himself. Upon returning to organized baseball, United States style, Mr. Maglie became the game's number-one pitcher in 1950. Starting in 16 games, Sal completed 12 while posting a mark of .750.

The 1950 greatness of Sal Maglie can be measured by his ability to hurl scoreless innings one on top of the other. The high mark for goose-eggs dished up in a row was Carl Hubbell's 46½ when Sal Maglie stepped to the mound on a damp and dreary day at the Polo Grounds to shoot at King Carl's lasting record. Gus Bell, Pirate rookie, almost put an end to Sal's skein in the very first inning by racing in from third base with a Pirate marker but the tag was put on galloping Gus by none other than bustling Maglie himself.

Later in the game this selfsame Gus Bell stepped to the platter against Maglie. Now Sal was just five putouts away from fracturing the consecutive scoreless stunt of Carl Hubbell.

Gus saw a curve breaking into him and more in self defense than anything else he fell back and took an unhealthy swing. The ball sailed away in the direction of the close-up right field stands. It actually was curving foul as it hit the pole for the cheapest of a long line of Chinese homers at the Polo Gounds. And by this quirk of fate, returned Mexican leaguer Sal Maglie lost his claim to fame!

Except for minor changes here and there in the rules, baseball has been played more or less under the same regulations throughout the modern period. Most important innovations have been in handling the sport, for example, playing ball at night under arc lights or bringing the game into homes via television.

Night baseball saw the light of light back in 1923 and came about quite by accident. Prior to that time, several unsuccessful attempts to play ball under artificial lighting had failed, at Fort Wayne, Indiana, as far back as 1883, at Cincinnati in 1899 and at Comiskey Park, Chicago, in 1918.

However, in 1923, the General Electric Company decided to open an athletic field for employees at

Lynn, Massachusetts, so company bigwigs arranged to string lights around the field for a gala nighttime celebration. Upon the scene converged a bunch of kids from the neighborhood carrying balls, bats and diamond equipment necessary for a game.

Startled company officials watched the game and came up with an idea. Why not night baseball in organized baseball, they asked? Experiments in more powerful illuminating systems followed and under a battery of 72 floodlights baseball's big night game was played satisfactorily.

Then in 1935, along came Col. Larry MacPhail to bring night ball to the majors and it was said that more than 14 games per season would ruin the novelty and kill the stunt.

One of MacPhail's staunchest opponents of night baseball had been Clark Griffith, volatile owner of the Washington Senators. After battling MacPhail tooth and nail against arclight baseball, Griffith changed his opinion completely and spurred by rising receipts under dark he became the first major mogul to campaign for baseball under the stars every day except Sundays. By 1949, about one-third of all baseball was played at night and, particularly in the minors, the number of arc tilts continues to increase. Few minor loops venture to play daytime contests anymore, except on Saturdays, Sundays or holidays.

The lush post-World War II days at an end, major league owners began retrenching in 1949 by dropping a total of 28 farm clubs. The figure increased in 1950 and threatened to grow worse by 1951. Television seemed to be the demon responsible for the demise of the minor leagues. Former solid financial franchises in Jersey City and Newark disappeared due to television reaching Jersey from big-league teams across the river in New York and Brooklyn.

In 1948, before throwing in the towel, the Newark Bears had a hot pennant contender in the International League, sticking in the thick of the pennant chase right down to the wire. Yet, in 1948 the Bears could attract only little better than 170,000 fans to their home park, Ruppert Stadium. Who can blame the franchise for quitting in disgust when bush-league cellar-dwellers were doing nearly as well at the gate?

Before the 1951 season got under way, minor-league teams were calling it quits in alarming numbers. True, much of the blame can be placed on the armed forces which were stripping the nation of its available healthy youth. Proponents of baseball broadcasting claim beaming of big-league games into minor-league cities via radio stimulates the sport there rather than harms it. This may be true, but television is something else. Given the opportunity of watching major-league play for free or minor-leagues play for pay, the average fan will choose the majors. If television continues, it seems baseball may develop into a sort of survival of the fattest.

Rare Diamond Gems

Away back around 1909, a fellow named Neal Ball
of Cleveland, known at that time as the Cleveland
Naps, startled the baseball world by pulling an un-
assisted triple play. Here's how he did it.

Cy Young was on the mound pitching for Cleveland against the Red Sox at League Park in Cleveland.
Second-sacker of the Sox, Amby McConnell, lashed
at a Young serve and sent a sizzling line drive in the
direction of center field. Leaping at the crack of the
bat, practically, Neal Ball pulled down the ball and
landed on second base doubling up the runner who
had left the station. The base-runner from first
crashed into Ball and he too was out, thereby com-
pleting the three-killing!

Other players since who have accomplished a similar play have been Bill Wambsganns, for Cleveland
against Brooklyn in the 1920 World Series; George
Burns for the Boston Red Sox against the Indians in
1923; Ernie Padgett for the Boston Braves against the
Phillies in the same year; Glenn Wright for Pittsburgh
against St. Louis, 1925; Jim Cooney for the Chicago
Cubs against Pittsburgh in 1927, and Johnny Neun
for Detroit against Cleveland in 1927 also.

Sometimes baseball can be the dangerous game. A
bolt of lightning in Pennsylvania once killed two outfielders running to field a batted ball. Back in 1940

Venezuela and Santo Domingo almost went to war after Venezuela won an important game on a close play in the ninth inning. Diplomatic relations actually were severed.

Before today's batter curses his luck too strongly, he should consider the case of Brooklyn relief pitcher Clarence Mitchell who came to bat twice in one game of the 1920 World Series against Cleveland and made five outs. Mitchell had the miserable misfortune to hit into one double-play and one triple-play!

As far as high hitting marks go, Monte Cross of the 1904 Athletics never set any. As a matter of fact, weak-willow Monte compiled the lowest major-league batting average ever for a regular, hitting .182 in 153 games. Sparkling shortstop Joe Cronin had the sort of tough luck few would like to experience by hitting into a triple play on a ball he kissed right on the nose. Joe's liner with the bases loaded hit third baseman Sammy Hale smack on the forehead, caroming into the waiting hands of shortstop Billy Knickerbocker who converted it into a three-ply killing.

One of the most profitable jobs in baseball belonged to pitcher Paul Schreiber when he was with the Yankees. A flop as a big-leaguer in his younger days, Schreiber the elder used to draw down about $8,500 a year although he was not even a member of the team. The big chucker, you see, was Yankee batting practice pitcher and he always came in for his share of first-place money.

Probably the greatest hitter in modern baseball records was the Georgia Peach, Ty Cobb. Yet, for all his ability with the willow, tough and ready Ty never was much of a power slugger. In only one season, 1909, did Ty top his league in home runs and his four-ply production for that semester was an uninspiring total of nine. Yet you must doff the hat to the Georgia Peach for his all-around ability at the plate. He failed to bat .300 or better only once in a career that covered 24 years!

Brooklyn newspaper man Nino Lo Bello comes up with some astounding big-league scores which will probably stand as records as long as the pyramids of Egypt. He points to the year 1902 when on July 14 a fellow by the name of Jay "Nig" Clarke hit eight home runs in one game for Corsicana in the Texas League. Final score of the game was 51-3. Going back further, the writer refers to October 20, 1865, the occasion when Al Reach of the Philadelphia Athletics scored 34 times in a twin bill, the unbelievable scores of these two contests being 100-8 and 162-11. (Somebody needed relief pitchers!)

Two of the best educated managers to guide major-league nines have been Eddie Sawyer, a Doctor of Philosophy and Phi Beta Kappa member who piloted the Phillies and Red Rolfe, Dartmouth graduate cum laude as well as former Detroit Tiger skipper. Probably the most versatile player to appear in the big show during recent years has been Mike Ryba, in later years a Cardinal coach. Ryba played every position on the field during his career, considering it commonplace to pitch the first game of a doubleheader and to catch the second.

Have a bit of pity for the immortal George Sisler. In a colorful career that saw George become one of the most skillful first-basemen in history with the St. Louis Browns over a 13-year stretch, he also proved a valuable man with the wood, maintaining a lifetime average of close to .350. Yet, for all his wonderful work George never had the opportunity of participating in World Series play.

Here's an odd one for you. Wake Forest College used a mechanical pitching machine in a ball game with North Carolina State College and won the game, 8-0. Not so fortunate as the automatic arm was A. Duggan, a chucker for Brown University, who fanned exactly 29 men in a nine-inning game only to lose a 1-0 heartbreaker.

Pitcher Bill Voiselle had an odd rookie record. Breaking in with the Giants of 1944, big Bill won a more than satisfactory 21 games although he contrived to give up 31 home runs, 13 more than any other National League pitcher. More curious, naturally, was the record of one Charlie "Bumpus" Jones. Bumpus the pitcher won but one big-league game and that, strangely, was a no-hit contest for Cincinnati.

What do you have to do to please your boss? After coming within a single point of copping the American League batting championship, infielder Tony Cuccinello drew his release the very next season from the White Sox. The Chicago neighbor, the Cubs, acted during the same season to cut pitcher Paul Derringer although the ace right-hander had marked up 16 wins in the previous campaign.

They say Smead Jolley was just about the worst outfielder in the history of baseball and events seem to bear out the charges. On one fine afternoon, Smead, a good hitter, made three errors on one hit ball while patrolling the outer garden for the White Sox. When a single was drilled Smead's way in left field, he allowed the ball to roll between his outstretched legs for one error. The ball then bounced off the fence and rolled once again through Smead's legs for error number two. Throwing the ball to home, Jolley committed his third miscue by pegging the pellet wildly right into the dugout!

King Carl Hubbell spent his entire major-league career with one team, the New York Giants. Carl set a modern major-league pitching mark by wrapping up 24 games in a row, his last 16 in 1936 and first eight in 1937. In his best season, 1936, King Carlos notched 26 victories against only six setbacks. In 1929 he twirled a no-hit game. Left-hander Carl Hubbell, natch, made Baseball's Hall of Fame.

Frankie Frisch, who once managed the Chicago Cubs, has always been widely recognized for his ability to put up a stiff tiff with any umpire within shouting distance. Yet, back in the days when Frankie was managing the Pirates he intervened on behalf of an umpire at an important National League meeting when it appeared the man in blue might have lost his job over an incident involving the Pirates. Off the field Frisch was everybody's friend.

Did you know that William Howard Taft, 26th President of the United States, was a catcher with the famous Cincinnati Red Stockings until he hurt his arm permanently. . . . Joe E. Brown was a promising ballplayer until he switched successfully to the field of comedy. . . . Abraham Lincoln was playing base-

ball when a committee came to inform him that he
had been nominated for the Presidency. Oh yes, he
took his last lick at bat before he left the game.

Here are some interesting statistics: There are
something like 12 million possible plays in baseball,
according to most recent mathematical calculations.
A typical fast-ball delivered by a pitcher travels ap-
proximately between 140 and 145 feet per second, or
94 to 98 miles per hour. A pitched ball, incidentally,
reaches the catcher in three-fifths of a second. And a
baseball has 109 stitches—108 on the outside and one
underneath the cover. (Now let someone tell you the
batter can count the stitches on a knuckle-ball delivery!)

Some of the more famous nicknames in major-
league history have been Connie Mack for Cornelius
McGillicuddy, Muggsey and The Little Napoleon for
John McGraw, The Georgia Peach for Ty Cobb, The
Flying Dutchman for Honus Wagner, The Gray
Eagle for Tris Speaker, The Big Six for Christy Mathewson, The Iron Horse for Lou Gehrig, The Big Train
for Walter Johnson, The Yankee Clipper for Joe
DiMaggio, The Man for Stan Musial and so on. Seems
as though a guy can't achieve baseball stardom until
sports writers hang a tag on him.

In modern records the Chicago Cubs and Philadelphia Phils hold the high mark for aggregate runs
scored in one game with 49 on August 25, 1922. The
Cubs, by the way, hold the single-inning high with
18 on September 6, 1883. Leaders in the triple-play
department for a single season are the Detroit Tigers
of 1911 and the Boston Red Sox of 1924, each of whom

engineered three such accomplishments in one year's play.

Mel Ott probably created one of the greatest sessions of second guessing in history when, as manager of the New York Giants in 1945, he ordered dangerous Bill Nicholson of the Cubs walked with the bases loaded. Here's one for the books: Nine railroad stops along the Missouri Pacific Railroad are named Miller, Admire, Allen, Bushong, Comiskey, Rapp, Helmick, Wisley and Delevan—which was the batting order of the old Chicago White Sox.

Baseballs today cost money and the average club keeps a pretty critical eye on the supply. During the 1950 season the St. Louis Browns had a bill for more than $13,000 for baseballs alone. It's small wonder the management discourages players from tossing baseballs into the stands, no matter how hard the fans plead.

It's odd that talented first-sacker Eddie Waitkus should have been laid low by the bullet from a gun pointed at him by a befuddled bobby-soxer. During the war years Eddie served in the Pacific and escaped unscathed in spite of his risky assignment as a sergeant machine-gun leader who flushed Japs out of the jungles for two years!

Although his batting style was technically wrong— he held his hands apart when he wrapped them around a bat—Ty Cobb stands out as the greatest hitter in the history of the game. His .367 average in over 3,000 games speaks for itself. In case you may have forgot, the Georgia Peach once stole 96 bases in a single season.

Baseball players do some crazy things. When Gabby Street was still a catcher he caught a ball thrown from the top of the Washington Monument. Have another oddity. The immortal Chicago Cub infield of Tinker-to-Evers-to-Chance, noted for its ability at executing the twin killing, appeared in four World Series between 1906 and 1910 and never once came up with a double-play in any of those contests!

Another war hero is American League pitcher Gene Bearden who has a silver plate in his head, the result of a serious wound suffered in World War II when the USS Helena was blown up by a Jap submarine in the Pacific. Correct name for former star Red Sox infielder Johnny Pesky is Paseskovich, but actually he's a Pesky hitter. Casualty lists show that catcher Edward Leneve, 22, of the Cubs' Visalia team in the Class C California League was the first professional baseball player killed in the Korean war. He met death on December 2, 1950, in Marine action between Udanammi and Huguriri.

Probably baseball's biggest mound workhorse was a fellow named Slim Haynes who hurled three shutouts in one day for the Stavely Club of Alberta, Canada. What's more, Slim toiled for more than 30 years in a Stavely uniform. Away back in 1909 a pitcher by the name of Durham with the Indianapolis team pitched and won five doubleheaders during the season. "Iron Man" Joe McGinnity, by the bye, pitched both games of a double-header five times during his career with the Giants. No doubt the greatest flash in the pan of all time was one Joe Borden who pitched baseball's first no-hit game in 1875. Borden finished the season in the big leagues, though, as a ground-keeper in Boston.

In spite of the chronic second-division clubs in baseball, most teams are rather evenly matched on the field. Statistics for a recent single season show that one out of every three games played in the majors—184 in the American League and 223 in the National League—were decided by one run. When Bill Kelly, later manager of Los Angeles, played in the International League he established himself as somewhat of a home-run hitter. With Minneapolis in 1927 he crowned all achievements by blasting out no less than five home runs in one game against St. Paul.

Greatest of baseball's screwball characters probably was immortal Rube Waddell. When Waddell caught up with his first big-league team, Louisville of the National League in 1897, he insisted on reporting to manager Fred Clarke at two o'clock in the morning. The peculiar rookie then went ahead and pounded on every hotel door, awakening sleepy players and introducing himself. Only one player refused to respond and the Rube was considerably hurt until he learned the innocent offender was Dummy Hoy, famous deaf-mute outfielder.

Speaking of trades, pitcher Joe Martina was acquired by the New Orleans Pelicans for a sack of oysters and first baseman Jack Fenton was bought by San Francisco for a carton of prunes. One of the few modern-day big-leaguers not born in the USA is Bobby Thomson of the Giants, a native of Glasgow, Scotland. Nick Altrock got credit for a victory with the White Sox, although he didn't throw a single pitch.

Hugh Casey, in a World Series game with the Dodgers, made just one delivery against the Yankees, yet was given credit for the win.

While in high school, Danny McFayden (later a star with the Braves) struck out 31 batters in a single ball game yet lost. In one ball game pitcher Guy Hecker picked John Stricker of the Athletics off first base three times in a row. (How careless can a guy get?) Since the beginning of baseball time, the New York Giants have won more baseball games than any other National League team. The figure is over 4,000.

In a game against the St. Louis Browns, Bud Clancey of the 1930 White Sox played first base without making a single play, assist or putout—and he wasn't asleep at the sack. Rivalry was so keen in a crucial series at the Polo Grounds back in 1919 that the Cincinnati Reds actually carried around their own water supply. Back in 1891 William Robinson, St. Louis Browns keystoner, had seven chances to handle and he committed seven errors.

Every fan thinks he knows his baseball—and he usually does. But baseball is such a big sport, a sport with such a rich history, none of us can know everything about the game and about those assorted performers who participate year after year in the national pastime.

Take for example a place like American League headquarters. From this inner sanctum once yearly comes an order to send a diver to the bottom of the Delaware River for the purpose of securing mud which is used to rub the shine off new baseballs each season. Your major league executive offices will also inform you that the 20 clubs in both circuits travel more than 200,000 miles per year!

Probably the champ workhorse of the baseball mound was appropriately named "Old Hoss" Charles Radbourne. He holds two unbelievable marks—one of 22 consecutive games pitched and another of 60 wins during a single season! Chucker Bill Voiselle, it might interest you to know, wore number 96 on his uniform no matter where he was playing. Reason? Well, Willy comes from a town name of Ninety-Six, South Carolina.

Billy Herman of the Cubs, Dodgers, Braves and Pirates is known as one of the National League's all-time slicksters around second. Yet, at the age of 18 Billy the kid pitched his New Covenant Presbyterian Sunday School team to the championship in Louisville amateur baseball. Then there's Cy Young, conceded to be the best pitcher ever to pick up a big-league glove, who did not hurl a shutout until he was well along into his third season. Over a period of 22 years Cy won 511 games.

And so it goes. Take the case of Umpire Beans Reardon. Oddly enough he never played in organized baseball. From the tender age of 16 Beans was calling balls and strikes in sandlot games. Actually, very few people question the integrity of umpires. Up until 1882, though, baseball umpires used to take testimony in close plays from spectators and players before making any important decision.

Cinderella Team

[CINDERELLA AND PRINCE CHARMING]

Every Cinderella must have a Prince Charming and baseball's National League pennant winners of 1951— the Giants—had theirs. The Prince Charming of the Cinderella Giants was a tall Scot from Staten Island, New York, named Bobby Thomson.

It was Bobby who smote the crushing ninth inning home run which sank the previously high-flying Brooklyn Dodgers and brought the New Yorkers their first flag in fourteen long and barren years. When Bobby belted Ralph Branca, for that long home run, one wit called it "the Scot heard 'round the world."

The success of the 1951 Giants is miraculous on two accounts. One was the humiliating, staggering eleven-game losing streak the team suffered early in the season to plunge it deep into the National League cellar; the other was the 13½ lead the Dodgers enjoyed over the Giants as late as August. For manager Leo Durocher's crew to overcome such odds reads like something from a story book—such as Cinderella, for example.

For his mass manipulations of player personnel, Leo the Lip earned himself the title, "Manager of the Year." In fact, little Leo notched the Associated Press honor by a landslide, drawing 113 votes to almost double the number gathered by his closest competitor, Casey Stengel, leader of the American League pennant winning Yanks, who grabbed 64 ballots. Stengel was 1950's "Manager of the Year."

The title awarded to dapper Durocher was a tribute to the faith of New York Giant president, Horace Stoneham. In mid-season of 1948, Stoneham lured the controversial skipper away from the Dodgers and dropped a bombshell on the baseball world. Friends and foes warned Stoneham about the consequences of such drastic action. But Leo the Lip came through for his boss, boosting the Giants in league standings until at last he earned—though the hard way—his 1951 pennant.

Far-sighted Durocher seemed to have a vision of things to come during the spring training sessions of 1951 when he said: "Whitey Lockman is my first baseman. Monty Irvin will be my left-fielder."

Critics snickered. Whitey could never hold down first base, they said. And for a while the criticism seemed solid, for it wasn't long before Leo put Monty back on first and Lockman back in left field.

In abandoning his experiment, Durocher gave some hint of additional moves in the future, by saying, "I want to set the team this year as quickly as possible. I'm positive Whitey Lockman can play an acceptable first base in any emergency, but for the present Monty Irvin is our first-baseman."

Early in the season, Leo pulled his first of two startling switches. He brought Whitey Lockman in to play first base again and he sent Monty Irvin back to the outer pastures. Monty did not seem to be able to adjust himself to first and his mistakes appeared to affect his batting eye. Leo knew the Giants needed power like Irvin gave promise of displaying in order to make a good showing.

In a way it pained Durocher to juggle his team in such fashion, but the eleven-game losing streak dictated drastic action. Leo's dreams of a fast start toward the pennant had faded and with it went strategy borrowed from the books of John McGraw. McGraw's plans were always directed in the direction of the quick getaway, a stroke that brought him ten pennants and eleven second-place finishes as head of the Polo Grounds crew for thirty long seasons.

Switch number two by Durocher occurred on May 25th when sensational, speedy, 20-year-old boy wonder Willie Mays took the centerfield position away from slumping Bobby Thomson. Following a slow start, Willie went on one of the maddest hitting sprees in Polo Grounds history. And when Willie wasn't hitting, he was fielding like a Tris Speaker with wings.

One play they'll talk about for years in Polo Grounds hot-stove league circles concerns a throw from centerfield by master Mays late in the season in an important game against the league-leading Dodgers. With his rifle arm, Willie broke the back of a Dodger rally and brought victory to the Giants in a crucial contest.

Willie took a fly-ball in not-too-shallow centerfield, executed a perfect spin and whipped the ball home to nip amazed Dodger third-sacker Billy Cox by plenty. Baseball writers and veteran fans called it the greatest throw ever witnessed in Polo Grounds history. No one stepped forward to dispute the contention.

Actually, Willie Mays was only part one of Durocher's switch number two. As with Monty Irvin, Leo figured he needed the latent power of Bobby Thomson. It pained the Giant pilot to see Br'er Bobby wasting away on the bench; it also pained Leo to observe the weak willow work of the incumbent Giant hot-corner guardian, Hank Thompson. Thus the stage was set for another Durocher manpower maneuver. He inserted Bobby Thomson at third base and he farmed Hank Thompson out to the minors.

Playing Don Mueller regularly in right field against both left and right-handed pitchers helped. Clint Hartung couldn't seem to level properly against the ball and his work as an outfielder left much to be desired. Magician Mueller, on the other hand, dropped bleeding hits with regularity beyond the outstretched fingers of irked outfielders and he handled the treacherous right-field Polo Grounds assignment with increasing confidence.

While an unbelieving world watched, the Giants made their move by winning 16 straight games in the latter part of the season. The victory skein represented the most productive stretch since 1935 when the Chicago Cubs rattled off 21 in a row.

The amazing thing about the Giant 16-straight mark was the fact that the team averaged less than five runs per game. Naturally, the Giant pitchers were superb, limiting the opposition to fewer than three tallies per contest. Jansen, Maglie, Hearn and Koslo bowled over the opposition with consummate ease. All told, the Giant hurling corps earned all-time respect by ticking off 41 victories in the last 50 starts of the season.

As the season moved along for the Giants, the early faith of Leo Durocher in Monty Irvin began to pay off ever increasingly. Leo himself echoed high praise for the quiet, hustling, Negro outfielder by saying on numerous occasions, "Every time I look up, Irvin is getting a key hit. Why he's been playing great ball all season, but no one seems to give him any credit."

And so it was. Even after Monty had attracted wide distinction for his standout play in the World Series, he lost out in the post-season "Most Valuable Player" balloting, as Brooklyn's star catcher Roy Campanella gained the award. Many disagreed, remembering how Irvin went on in amazing fashion to knock in more runs with his stick than any other player in the league despite an inauspicious start which saw the popular Orange New Jersey slugger bat across nary a run during the first two weeks of the campaign.

Monty went about setting himself a World Series record in the losing cause against the New York Yanks, which saw the Yankee Stadium steamroller squash the Giants four games to two. Irvin, the human howitzer, slapped out eleven hits in five games setting a mark for that number of contests. Monty also drew raves for his swipe of home during the early part of the Series when the Yanks were still playing like befuddled fogies. The Giants of 1951 did things in remarkable fashion—stealing home in a World Series game and lashing out a three-run homer in the bottom of the ninth of the final of three playoff games against

Brooklyn to win the pennant. No wonder they quickly earned the title of Cinderella team.

Monty Irvin, notwithstanding, it is extremely doubtful whether the Giants would have come close to the pennant at all without the services of Sal the Barber, better known around Niagara Falls, New York, as Sal Maglie. The Giant curve-ball specialist represents one of those curious cases—common to the pitching profession—of coming into his own when men who perform at the other eight positions are prepared to call it a career.

They say Sal Maglie learned to pitch during his hitch in the Mexican League, and he undoubtedly did, for in the minors prior to his Latin-American slab efforts, Sal had hardly been a ball of fire. In fact, his records at some minor-league whistle stops were so spotty, Maglie had several times almost decided to call it quits with baseball and to return to the field of shaves and hair cuts and bay rum.

Maglie's contribution to the N.Y. Giant 1951 pennant effort was a 23-6 mark, proving his 18-4 record of 1950 was no fluke. Thus in two seasons as a Giant, Sal accounted for the incredible number of 41 victories against a scant ten setbacks and it must be remembered he didn't become a starter until the 1950 season was well under way.

What did this quiet, dark student of the mound have on the ball? A curve, a curve and a curve is the answer. Maglie, you see, threw three different kinds of curves and they all confused the opposition. What's more, he was an unemotional character, cool as a Coke and rarely given to spells of wildness. His 1951 contribution to pennant victory is even more important in light of the fact that of Sal's 23 victories, five were "must" ones over the rough-tough Dodgers. On the other hand, the barber dropped only one tussle to the Brooks all season. In fact, one loss in two years was Maglie's Brooklyn record. Not since the days of Carl Hubbell, when the King won 26 in 1936 and 32 the following year, have the Giants come up with such a mound gem as Maglie.

That the Giants had the guts to rebound when the going was rough was proved by playoff game number three. In the second of the three sets, the Dodgers had walloped the Giants via a 10-0 victory behind rookie hurler Clem Labine. Such a shellacking would take the starch out of more than one ballclub. Then when the Brooks jumped into a 4-1 lead late in the third playoff game, you wouldn't have given an inflated sou for the chances of the men from Coogan's Bluff. But once again the Giants clawed back, thanks—as has been related countless times—to the three-run blast of terror Thomson.

King of the rebounders, no doubt, were the National League's other Cinderella men, George Stalling's "Miracle Braves" of 1914. As late as July 19 of that year, the Braves wilted in the National League cellar. Then to the amazement of all baseball fandom, the Braves started climbing until, with the aid of a whirlwind finish, they ultimately stitched up the National League flag.

No less unbelievable was their four-game sweep of the Philadelphia Athletics in the World Series that year. The Braves of 1914 and the Giants of 1951 will ever live in baseball history as the comeback cuties of all time.

As remarkable as was the 1951 pitching of Sal Maglie in the majors, just as eye-opening was the batting prowess of Willie Mays in the minors before he joined the Giants on May 25th. Down at the Minneapolis farm of the New York Giants, walloping Willie swatted the hard hide for a robust .477. Thus for more than one month of the Triple-A American Association season, Willie hit close to .500!

That Willie made the grade with the Giants while still a young whippersnapper of 20 is no accident. In school, Willie was good enough to cover centerfield for the highly rated Birmingham Black Barons of the Negro National League where Mays performed for two seasons.

After going one-for-26 in his major-league debut, Willie got his good eyes on the ball and blasted the pill all over every big league lot. Probably, Willie was just the spark the Giants needed for once he started hitting, the Polo Grounds gang started hitting on all eight (not including the pitcher, of course).

Eventually Willie went on a home-run hitting spree, the likes of which had not been seen by Giant fans since the hey-day of Mel Ott. Curiously, Willie was never a long-ball hitter before coming to the majors. In his two years with the Black Barons, Willie could manage no better than five homers a season and in his last lower-league semester before joining the Giants, at Trenton, Willie propelled the same number of four-baggers: five.

One of baseball's greatest all-time hitters paid Willie

Mays a top compliment after seeing the 1951 rookie in action for the first time. Said Al Simmons of Willie Mays: "He's the best kid ball player I've seen in years. Look at that stance at the plate and that poise in the field. You can't beat it."

When you rave of Giant pitching you must save a rave for the man behind the scenes, coach Frank Shellenback the man who has guided several of the Giant flippers to a healthier win column and a leaner loss one. Jansen, Maglie, Hearn, et al all give credit to Shellenback's slab wisdom. Small wonder then, that Giant players affectionately refer to Shellenback as "The Pitching Doctor."

Shellenback, in his prime, was a top-flight pitcher in the minors, although he never clicked in the majors. That Frank failed to make the grade in the big show was due to a terrible stroke of fate. The Chicago White Sox had been high on Frank and were ready to give him his chance at stardom in 1919 when the spitball pitch suddenly was outlawed. Shellenback, you see, was a spitball pitcher almost exclusively. Only those already in the majors were permitted to continue throwing the spitter.

So brilliant was the minor-league mark of Frank Shellenback during the next ten years, Connie Mack made a serious bid for the hurler in 1930. Everything in the deal hinged on whether Shellenback would be able to use his Pacific Coast League spitball in the American League. At length, the league voted against it and Shellenback was thus denied his last opportunity for fame and fortune in the big leagues.

However, in the persons of his star students, Maglie,

Hearn and Jansen, the Shellenback touch not only made the big leagues but the World Series of 1951.

The home run pitch tossed by Branca to Thomson brings to mind another round-tripper served to Babe Ruth by no less a personage than Dazzy Vance. Aside from being one of the most colorful men in baseball, Vance was also one of the best paid. Vance of the Brooks stopped off with his team in Atlanta, Georgia, for an exhibition game against Ruth and his Yanks.

In no time at all, the Yanks filled the bases and up stepped Babe Ruth. Dazzy Vance quietly surveyed the situation, then blew a fast one down the middle. Just as neatly, Babe Ruth knocked the serve right out of the ballpark. Naturally, Dazzy got the hook.

After a short shower, Dazzy joined his brother who had been watching the game from the stands. Asked the brother: "Is it true you get $25,000 a year for this?"

Vance nodded.

In amazement, the brother shook his head. "I never saw a man make so much money so easy."

Speaking of pitchers, one must speak of Big Jim Hearn. Giant skipper Durocher got his first look at the blaze-ball righthander while on a USO tour through Manila. Hearn was in the service in those days and after his discharge, he migrated to the Cardinals. Durocher liked the stuff displayed by Hearn while pitching GI ball, so it's only natural he snapped at the chance to buy the sometimes wild righthander for a modest fee after St. Louis gave up on the big fellow.

Originally, an outfielder, Hearn came to pitching quite by accident. He had been covering centerfield for the Macon, Georgia, team when the club ran out of pitchers. Because of promise he had shown during batting practice twirling, big Jim was pressed into service. For nine innings of his first start, Hearn tossed two-hit, shutout ball. However, he lost the game in the eleventh when his second-baseman let a pop fly fall safe with a runner in scoring position.

The accidental mound start launched Jim Hearn on a career, heavy with heartbreak, but finally smashing success as he bested the Brooklyns in the first of the 1951 playoff games and capped by a World Series victory over the Yanks, although Sheldon Jones came to his rescue.

At that, Hearn earned a notable distinction. He became the first Giant righthander to beat the Yanks since Hal Schumacher turned the trick away back in 1936.

All in all, it can be said that Scot Bobby Thomson was the man who broke Brooklyn's back in more ways than one. In addition to propelling the home run that brought the Giants their victory flag, Bobby smacked Dodger hurling for a grand total of eight home runs, or exactly one-fourth of his entire 32 four-master output. Ralph Branca, who threw the home run ball to Thomson in the final playoff game, served three juicy gophers. Thomson hit two off Carl Erskine and one each off Preacher Roe, Don Newcombe and Phil Haugstad.

It will take the Giants a very long time to forget National League Season, 1951. The Dodgers, ditto!